Another Day at the Front

Another Day at the Front

DISPATCHES FROM THE RACE WAR

Ishmael Reed

BASIC
BOOKS

A Member of the Perseus Books Group
New York

54852522

Designed by *Brent Wilcox*

Library of Congress has cataloged the hardcover edition as follows:
Reed, Ishmael, 1938–
    Another day at the front : dispatches from the race war / Ishmael Reed
        p.   cm.
    Includes index.
    ISBN 0-465-06891-X (hc)
        1. United States—Race relations.   2. Racism—United States.
    3. African Americans—Civil rights.   4. Hispanic Americans—Social conditions.
    5. Muslims—United States.   I. Title.
    E184.A1 R426   2002
    305.8'00973—dc21
    Paperback ISBN 0-465-06892-8   2002010563

04 05 06 / 10 9 8 7 6 5 4 3 2 1

This book is dedicated to the memory of Calvin Hernton, Dr. Barbara Christian, Gwendolyn Brooks, Claude Brown, Abiola Sinclair, Thomas Flannagan, and Jos Knipscheer

Contents

Introduction

SHORTLY AFTER THE TERRORIST ATTACKS ON THE WORLD TRADE Center and the Pentagon, I received a call from Patrick Reardon of the *Chicago Tribune*. He wanted to know whether I thought that the civil liberties of Americans would be threatened as a result. I told him that African-Americans had lived under a police state for 300 years and that we were used to our civil liberties being threatened. During the antebellum period, the movements of blacks were monitored by the Slave Patrols, gangs of white thugs who often brutalized blacks on capricious pretexts.

African-Americans have been at war with some elements of the white population since the very beginning. Perhaps this is why Ogun and Shango are the most popular of all of the entities of the Yoruba pantheon, which the African faithful carried with them across the Atlantic. They are associated with war. Being African-American in this hemisphere has been a battle, and each day is like a day at the front. The battle styles include everything from megaaggression, full-scale race riots, and lynchings to microaggression, everyday rudeness, and humiliation.

In the United States, African-Americans have been on the receiving end of others' enmity from the time they arrived in this country, often getting the worst of it, but just as often, as the poet Claude McKay said in his great poem "If We Must Die," "fighting back" and succeeding against overwhelming odds. Blacks have been subjected to violence of the most cruel and macabre sort and have been targeted for physical and psychological aggression, from the street thugs who render random beatings to the sneers and ridicule from intellectuals, who are bought and paid for by wealthy corporate donors. The oligarchy that owns both the politicians and the media comforts "white America" by denigrating African-Americans and ignoring or downplaying the flaws of whites. Andrew Hacker, a man who plays Asian-Americans against African-Americans, even said in the *New York Review of Books* (Oct. 7, 1993) that whites don't engage in personal violence. It's a black thing.

When James Atlas commented that slaughter on American soil is rare, or when Judy Woodruff of CNN said that the WTC was only the second terrorist attack on American soil, I was wondering which version of American history they had read. Blacks have been massacred and bombed on American soil. In this book, I have included my review of Anthony Grooms's book, *Bombingham*, which is about the terror campaign waged against Birmingham blacks during the 1950s.

Even whites who've been seen as sympathetic to blacks have been terrorized. In 1863, a Confederate named William Clarke Quantrill and his band of drunken comrades massacred 150 men, women, and children in Lawrence, Kansas. Their crime? That of being "negro lovers." Among this murderous gang was Frank James, brother of Jesse, both of whom continue to be lionized in Hollywood, without anybody on the right complaining about this distortion of the public record.

Up to now, people bearing a white skin have been the chief tormentors of African-Americans (and no matter how much neoconservatives make of the crack epidemic that influenced black-on-black homicide in the 1980s, white men killed more black men in the twentieth century than did black men).

With the rise of the Hispanic and Asian-American populations, there may come a time when African-Americans will wax nostalgic about the good old days when white racism was their only concern.

Though African-Americans have made alliances with other minority groups, many immigrants and native-born people of other colors may join the forces of white racism, which is how preceding generations of immigrants acquired a "whiteness" upgrade. Using "whiteness" to get ahead. In the last election, 70 percent of American Muslims, including those from India, Pakistan, and North Africa, voted for the Republicans, a party that has, in the last few decades, been viewed by many African-Americans as hostile to their interests. This statement may come as a surprise to those who have associated me with "multiculturalism," but just because my associates and I have been connected with writers and artists of different ethnic backgrounds since the 1960s doesn't mean that such intellectual camaraderie can be transmitted to the street level. Indeed, at the height of the Nazi terror, there were Jewish and German writers who were communicating. When I visited Israel, I learned that regardless of the mad policies of the politicians and theocrats in the Middle East, and the violence between Palestinians and Israelis, Jewish and Arab writers were meeting and discussing issues.

For admission to the white fraternity, stomping on blacks seems to be required of immigrants to the United States. This is nothing new, and African-American writers from the time of David Walker have commented about how new immigrants have been treated better that African-Americans. The immigrants are often praised at the expense of African-Americans, and the "pathologies" occurring in immigrant communities, like those of whites, are often ignored by the media and policymakers. For example, the highest rate of "out-of-wedlock" births in Oakland, California, is among Southeast Asian women and the highest school dropout rate is among Samoans.

Richard Rodriguez commented in *Salon* about how "Hispanics" are being divided from African-Americans.

> All is not well along the spectrum of America's rainbow, despite
> the tendency of some on the political left to describe "blacks and

Latinos" in one breath. From Miami to Dallas to Compton, blacks
and Latinos are engaged in a terrible competition for the meanest
jobs; for the security of Civil Service positions; for political office;
for white noise. It is no exaggeration to say that African-Americans
have paid the price of Hispanic numerical ascendancy. In Los
Angeles, for example, the famous "black neighborhoods" have
suddenly become Hispanic—immigrant, Spanish-speaking.

Recently, a Hispanic man killed a black man because he objected to black men mingling with women of his "race," the leading
cause of psychosis among white racists. Some Hispanics have committed hate crimes against blacks, and a few are members of the
Klan. The Hispanic-black feud is often the result of the white establishment's dividing the two groups for its own pernicious
agenda. For example, why does the census use racial categories
when it comes to blacks and whites, but when it comes to "Hispanics" uses a European linguistic category? What do the people
whom we call Hispanics have to do with Europe? The Spanish
scholars with whom I met in Madrid don't consider the Hispanics
to be European. There was very little intermingling between the
Spanish (Andalusians, the conquistadors who, to this day, are considered the "niggers" of Spain) and indigenous Indian women.
Moreover, millions of those whom we call "Hispanics" have
"African blood." Since the United States operates on the "one-drop
rule" (one drop of "African blood" defines you as black), the invention of those who merchandised in human beings, why aren't these
millions of Hispanics considered African-Americans? After new
census figures pointed to the rise of the "colored" population and
the dwindling of the "white" one, Harvard Professor Orlando Patterson rushed onto the op-ed pages of the *New York Times* to assure
whites that they had nothing to worry about ceasing to be the majority, because millions of Hispanics are white.

His op-ed and opinions were received by the *Times* and National Public Radio, which exclude the opinions of Mumia Abu-

Jamal, because both media outfits are in the same business as the Talented Tenth, of which Patterson is a charter member: comforting mainstream opinion. Patterson and his friends are followers of the W. E. B. DuBois of *The Souls of Black Folk*. Like DuBois felt at one time, they believe that if blacks will just shape up, and assimilate, attend the opera, whites will associate with them and accept them. Of course, DuBois also believed that integration would be achieved in his lifetime but, ultimately, came to the conclusion that white racism was, in John A. Williams's words, "an inexorable force." Almost immediately, Orlando Patterson, who believes with some of his Talented Tenth colleagues that the woes of black Americans are self-inflicted, was challenged by Miriam Jimenez Roman and Gina Perez, two researchers at the Center for Puerto Rican Studies at Hunter College of the City University of New York. They called Patterson's analysis flawed. "That Latinos are not considered true whites is evident by their classification as Hispanic whites, a conditional whiteness bestowed on (or claimed by) only some (and not all, as Mr. Patterson suggests)." With hope, a Hispanic-African-American alliance will be formed. In the 2001 New York primary, a Puerto Rican mayoral candidate was supported by a black–Puerto Rican coalition. In Los Angeles, however, many blacks voted against the Hispanic candidate in favor of a white candidate, who double-crossed them, shortly after the election, by firing a popular black police chief.

Some Hispanics aren't the only ones who share the racist attitudes of some whites toward blacks. Blacks want to know why the terrorists who destroyed the World Trade Center and a section of the Pentagon were treated so well and had such a nice time during their stay in the United States, enjoying all of the privileges of citizenship. Some were enrolled in flight school, others attended universities, at a time when some universities are abandoning affirmative action programs. My lawyer, Howard Moore. Jr., said that he'd probably have to sue in order to gain admission for blacks into those flight schools. This wouldn't be the first time that the enemies of the United States received better treatment than African-Americans.

In a special issue of my zine, *Konch*, devoted to the responses of thirty-eight writers to the WTC bombing, Marvin X, an African-American playwright, complained about Arab-Americans peddling pork, alcohol, and crack in black neighborhoods. In Oakland, California, members of an African-American Muslim group, led by Minister Yusef Bey, and Arab-American mom-and-pop store owners have almost come to blows over these practices. Some Arab-American store owners have also been accused of exchanging credit for sexual favors with black women customers, according to Marvin X. My oldest daughter, Timothy, a novelist (*Showing Out*), who lived for some years in Bed-Stuy, verifies this. There are many African-Americans who believe that some Arab-Americans are as racist as some whites; therefore, it's not surprising that blacks, in a national poll, favored the racial profiling of Arab-Americans in overwhelming numbers, without many of them realizing that in the eyes of some whites, they also could be classified as Arab, a subject that I address in the essay "The Rest of Us Are Arab."

Are there black racists? Of course there are, and the media, which serve as the chief arm of white nationalist propaganda, joyfully reward the blacks who make anti-white and anti-Semitic statements with considerable coverage, as a way of attracting viewers to their vile products and providing whites with entertainment, while embarrassing blacks. This is not only true of the corporate media but also public radio, which black journalist Amy Alexander, a contributor to Africana.com, accuses of liberal racism. The basketball star Charles Ward made some anti-Semitic remarks and was roundly condemned by *New York Times* writers. But the coverage of racism among some Jewish intellectuals, a subject that the *Times* promised Henry Louis Gates Jr. that it would cover, as a companion to his piece portraying blacks as anti-Semites, never appeared. That's too bad, because in my examination of *The Turner Diaries*, the bible of the white ultra-right, I've found that white extremists target both blacks and Jews. If we condemn black anti-Semites for mouthing similar rhetoric, then shouldn't some of the Jewish commentators and artists be questioned about their use of racist rhetoric against blacks? In his review of the film *Ali*, which included a blatant attack on the Nation of Islam, Robert Lipsyte used the term "hoodoo Islam," a slight at not only Islam, but also at African indigenous religion, and no one complained. Blacks are depicted by places like Fox News, whose president is Roger Ailes, the designer of the infamous Willie Horton ad, as so thin-skinned and P.C. Yet no black organization threw up a picket line to complain about Lipsyte's slur.

Black racism is just one of the issues that both the corporate and alternative media use to ridicule blacks in order to please their target audience: white males, many of whom are angry. Marvin Kalb of the Shorenstein Center at Harvard admitted to a questioner, during an appearance on C-Span, that the media were racist, because their target audience was white males.

On the other hand, white racism is receiving gentle treatment. Some of the media are even giving the Confederacy a second look and deciding that they like what they see. NPR's Scott Simon, for example, leads the tributes for the neo-Confederacy, praising terrorists and mass murderers like General Nathan Bedford Forrest and Stonewall Jackson and comparing the retreat of the Confederate army from Richmond with the long march at Bataan. Simon, Shelby Foote, and Tony Horowitz, author of *Confederates in the Attic*, praise Robert E. Lee, a man who carried out the policy, set by the Confederate congress, that black soldiers caught fighting on the side of Union troops be shot on the spot.

American politics and culture have become so topsy-turvy that black men, who mobilized the population to defeat the old black codes, through marches and demonstrations, are now blamed for the problems of blacks in American society. Even Pacifica radio, a valuable progressive outfit, gives considerable air time to white male progressives and black and white feminists who depict black men as the walking emblems of all mistreatment of women. Yet, according to my examination of the treatment of women in other American ethnic groups, the treatment of women by black men is no worse than their treatment by males of other groups, and in some cases better. While the murder of white women by their boyfriends and husbands has remained the same, the murder of black women by their boyfriends and husbands *has declined by 40 percent since 1976.* Nor do I know any of the brothers who advocate arranged marriages.

Moreover, it has been my experience that among American racial and ethnic groups, African-Americans have been the most compassionate, and the most devoted to justice and freedom, even when their positions have made them unpopular with their fellow countrymen and women. They're the ones who stood up when the recent presidential election was stolen in Florida, a repeat of the centennial election of 1876, when roadblocks were set up in Florida to prevent blacks from voting, and the sites of balloting were switched, and two Supreme Court decisions sided with those who sought to deny blacks the franchise. They're the ones who stand up and fight back when modern-day patrollers use the badge as a shield and shoot down unarmed black men in the streets. And though many women ran and were elected by using Anita Hill's alleged problems with Clarence Thomas as a rallying cry, Senator Carol Mosely Brown, a black woman, was the only woman senator to vote against Bill Clinton's welfare reform bill, which has made the situation of poor women, most of whom are white, even worse. The Bush administration's mad, reckless dash into Afghanistan was opposed by a black woman, Congresswoman Barbara Lee. She had the courage to remind the country that it's the job of Congress to declare war. Moreover, while the mainstream gay and lesbian organizations supported the Bush war polices and only complained when someone printed a scurrilous anti-gay remark on a missile, a group named for the late black writer Audre Lorde *complained about the actual bombing.* When I look at the polls in which most whites have endorsed an attack on civil liberties, advocated by our current neo-Confederate attorney general, I feel that it's black Americans who are the sentinels, who will fight to protect democracy from the encroachment of fascism on our country. They have a tradition of defending freedom, which for them is more than a concept, but an entity before which one makes offerings.

When Maxine Waters stands up and delivers her passionate stinging rebukes of racism, you're taken back to those old abolitionist halls where Sojourner Truth and Harriet Tubman made similar appeals. In this country, the fighters for justice and for fairness are most likely to be black and, for them, every day is another day at the front, regardless of their class and level of achievement. Even Tiger Woods in sports and Houston Baker Jr., a man with impeccable academic credentials, are subjected to racist taunts.

The essays in this book are about people on both sides of the front. Among them are Quincy Troupe and William Pierce, a.k.a. Andrew McDonald, in the present, Booker T. Washington and John Calhoun in the past.

Senator John C. Calhoun was one of the best educated people of his time. A Yale graduate, he was the leading proponent of minority rights, even if the rights he defended were the rights of slave owners to traffic in and enslave human beings. Though some consider Calhoun's ideas to be out-of-date, it is my opinion that Calhounism defines the spirit of the contemporary United States. The current president, George W. Bush, refused to take a stand on whether South Carolina fly the Confederate flag, and his wife defended this symbol of a sovereign government, which fought to defend slavery. Bush also ran on a platform of state's rights (except when it came to a branch of the federal government deciding the presidential election on his behalf), the battle cry of John C. Calhoun, who described himself as a "merciful slavemaster." Moreover, two of Bush's cabinet members, Attorney General John Ashcroft and Interior Secretary Gale Norton, are champions of the Confederacy, and the Senate minority leader has cooperated with a pro-Confederate group.

No wonder autographs of John Wilkes Booth, a Confederate hero, are selling for more than the autographs of Abraham Lincoln. Maybe, fifty years from now, someone will erect a statue to John Wilkes Booth in the capital if this neo-Confederate trend continues.

Rather than being out-of-style, John Calhoun is hip nowadays. And so is the Confederate flag. While some white Southerner's cherish the Confederacy with obvious signals like Confederate flags flying from the back of pickup trucks, Northern intellectuals, often former radicals, take a more subtle approach. Both the *New York Times Magazine* and the *Southern Partisan* are devoted to the faith that Western civilization is under attack by the forces of diversity. Calhoun's example shows that even the most enlightened and intellectual individuals hold views that are no different from any backwoods peasant (who at least gave us the blues and country-western music). Indeed the most racist book of this period, *The Turner Diaries*, was written by a physicist. One can understand the myths about race promoted by the corporate media, out to make profits from white resentment, but when such junk shows up among the hippest of whites, one becomes pessimistic about the future of race relations in this country. For example, I've found that some of the most progressive and educated feminists share the attitudes of Calhoun toward blacks.

In the May/June 2001 issue of the *American Book Review*, a reviewer wrote that black and white middle-class feminists, with hundreds of years of graduate school between them, are shown to be prone to the same kind of ignorant thinking that has dogged black men for hundreds of years. In a review of *Rape on the Public Agenda: Feminism and the Politics of Sexual Assault*, by Maria Bevacqua, the reviewer, H. Kassia Fleisher, said that white feminists like Susan Brownmiller took the late Eldridge Cleaver's confession that he prepared for his rape of white women by practicing on black women to represent the experience of all black men. (Maria Bevacqua, *Rape on the Public Agenda*, 44–45) (Benjamin Schwarz used Cleaver to make the same generalization in a book review appearing in the *Los Angeles Times*. Schwarz justified the lynchings of black men by white Southern mobs on the grounds that they were probably guilty.) Moreover, feminist Ruth Rosen's singling out of the late Kwame Toure's statement that the position of women in SNCC was "prone" has also been used to smear black men. Toure said that he was merely reporting facts. Isn't this the kind of collective blame that has aroused resentment, persecution, and hate crimes against Jews for centuries? Using the example of an individual to smear a whole class? It wasn't a black man who battered author Betty Freidan so that she found it necessary to cover her wounds with makeup before appearing on television.

Why does Eldrige Cleaver represent the experience of all black men and not Ralph Ellison, Ralph Bunche, or Ralph Abernathy? Does Meyer Lansky represent the experience of all Jewish men? Timothy McVeigh, all Irish-American men? Lucky Luciano, Italian-American men?

According to Fleisher, Bevacqua accuses white middle-class feminists of using the scepter of the black rapist and aligning themselves with the Republican right to pass anti-rape legislation, just as nightriders and terrorists during the Reconstruction period used the phantom Black Rapist to justify genocidal actions against black people, using one group's scapegoating to advance the goals of another. This alliance has contributed to the high incarceration of black men who are seen as jeopardizing the safety of white women, a suburban myth. Bevacqua wrote "Fears of black criminality and underclass insurgency informed this [far right] agenda. Policy makers, wanting to appear tough on crime, saw the opportunity to support legislation being advanced by anti-rape activists advantageous. Thus political compromises with tough-on-crime legislators, coupled with the formalization and co-optation of anti-rape projects, have dulled the radical potential of the[feminist] movement."

Bevacqua accused Brownmiller of failing to address the issue of race in her "landmark" book *Against Our Will: Men, Women and Rape*. Wrong. In one of the most dishonest, vicious, and opportunistic passages, even for middle-class feminist thought, Brown-miller accuses Emmett Till, the black teenager who was murdered and mutilated by racist psychos, of getting what he deserved. His alleged offense? Wolf-whistling at this white woman. Brownmiller didn't end there. In a further passage she bonds with Till's killers, perhaps foreshadowing the alliance between white middle-class feminists and white males of the right that was to come. Brown-miller said that a few years later, after this crime, she was whistled at by some black men in New York and was beset by a "murderous rage." Now get this! White feminists who blamed Emmett Till for his death ignored the testimony from his mother. She said that she told her son, a stutterer, that whenever he was seized by an episode of stuttering that he should whistle to get attention. (Brownmiller, in her book, a feast of antipathy toward black men, also accused all black men of encouraging rape.)

Here is an example of how the white middle-class feminist movement treats its black sisters. They took the murderer's account of the incident over that of their black sister. Though black feminists complain about being excluded from the hierarchy of the feminist movement, black Divas, who depict black men as dogs, have found a huge market among white women consumers. In Kevin Powell's *Step Into A World*, a writer said that white women consumers do not empathize with the plight of black women characters in these harlequin melodramas, but substitute the experience of these black characters with their own. In other words, black men and women are used to channel conflicts that are held in secret by whites, sort of like Whoopie Goldberg's role in the movie *Ghost*. A study by SUNY–Buffalo, revealing a "horrific picture" of lives saturated with serious domestic violence, provides a concrete example of how the media and politicians and think tanks cover up problems in the white community until they burst out as Columbine and the bombing of the federal building in Oklahoma. The findings are part of a larger study funded by a $500,000 grant from the Spencer Foundation, which will be published by Beacon in 2003.

The study was conducted by Lois Weis, professor of education at the University of Buffalo, and Michelle Fine, professor of social psychology in the Graduate Center, City University of New York.

The researchers defined "serious domestic violence" as "battering intended to cause serious physical injury. *Ninety-two percent of white female respondents said that such domestic violence was directed against them, their mothers, and/or sisters, either in their birth households or in later relationships*" (my italics). By comparison, 62 percent of black female subjects reported similar levels of violence in their lives. Weis called the results "extremely disturbing. This does not mean that 92 percent of all white working-class women are, or have been, victims of serious domestic violence," she said. "*It does, however, suggest a far more serious problem in this population than has otherwise been acknowledged.*"

"Some women said they grew up in homes in which serious abuse was part of the fabric of their daily lives," she noted. "They described regular beatings of themselves, their mothers and sisters by other family members. Some spoke of being seriously abused in adult male-female relationships as well. Others described the violent, abusive relationships of one or more sisters." Weis said the results were especially surprising because the subjects in the study were not selected because the researchers believed them to be the worst off in their communities. "The . . . subjects were all members of relatively stable families and were involved in church, school or community organizations and activities," she said. She said that they found that the thirty-one black women respondents were much more open about the violence they saw and experienced.

"The white women in the study, on the other hand," she said, "were very secretive. *Weis speculated that such secretiveness serves to protect the popular image of family life in the white community!*" (My italics.) That the white community hides its dirt, while projecting it onto blacks comes as no secret to the generations of blacks who've worked in the homes of whites and carried tales back to the black community about what went on in these homes, as far

xxii   **Another Day at the Front**

back as plantation days when black house servants, who saw their mistresses strung out on cocaine, while their husbands tried to bed down every African woman in sight. For this book, I sent this study to white feminists at KPFA radio in Berkeley, California, National Public Radio, the *Oakland Tribune,* and Salon.com—outfits where black men are bashed, regularly. I asked them two questions: Why, in their opinion, didn't this study receive much media coverage and two, did they agree with Weis that "secretiveness serves to protect the popular image of family life in the white community"?

Only Susan Lydon of the *Oakland Tribune* answered my questions. The coverup continues. Both Susan Brownmiller and Gloria Steinem have made statements that are libelous of black men, but I haven't heard them condemn the treatment of Jewish women in Jewish households, a complaint made in almost every issue of *Lilith*, a Jewish feminist magazine. While visiting Israel, I learned that the incidence of crimes of homicide against women by their husbands is the highest in the West, so high that Prime Minister Barak commented about it. To confirm this, all one has to do is go to www.TheJerusalemPost.com and search "domestic violence."

Brownmiller and Steinem aren't the only ones who ignore the abuses of women in their ethnic background, while condemning the male members of another group. They're not the only ones who believe that all of the social problems are located in the black community. My white students at the University of California at Berkeley, who form their opinions about blacks from television and Hollywood, challenged me when I said that the typical crack addict is white. In fact, according the Centers for Disease Control and Prevention, white teenagers are seven times more likely to smoke crack and sell drugs than blacks.

I came to the conclusion, in the late eighties, that "a tangle of pathologies" existed in other communities, the only difference being that these problems, like the abuse of white women by white men reported by SUNY, were kept secret by the politicians, the media, and public intellectuals. They blame blacks while hiding their own dirty laundry.

Exaggerating the faults of the enemy and covering up those of the group that one champions is an old strategy in warfare. So sophisticated and hi-tech has become the denigration of African-Americans, the enemy, that even those of the intellectual population are influenced by such propaganda.

If politicians and the media had been examining white pathology as I had (gaining as much work as the Maytag repair man) perhaps the school massacres occurring in white schools could have been avoided. President Clinton, like his once adversary, now imitator, Jerry Brown, found support among the white population by getting tough with blacks.

He was one of those who participated in the act of protecting whites from their secrets. At a time when he was shoring up his base among Reagan Democrats, by lecturing blacks about their personal behavior, I wrote a piece, in 1994, for the *New York Times*, pointing to disturbing trends among youth in the suburbs and talking about how whites were complicit in the drug trade while the media were raising their revenue by blaming all drug dealing and crime on blacks in the inner city. I'd relied for my information upon studies that had been printed in the *Times* and elsewhere. President Clinton, who came to power by getting tough with blacks, while posing as a white Negro, was found to be wanting in his own personal life. But in fairness to him, he wasn't the only scolder of blacks who had higher standards for them than for himself. Indeed, David Brock, author of *Blinded by the Right*, revealed some of the most powerful media critics of the moral behavior of blacks and Clinton to be hypocrites in their own lives. While the media were blaming blacks, particularly black men, for all of the nation's problems, the Eurocentric cultural critics were inflaming public opinion with rumors about a black takeover of American campuses. James Atlas, a *Times* mainstay and Bellow biographer, seemed to think so. He reported in the *New York Times Magazine* and his book *The*

Book Wars that the Modern Language Association was being over-run by barbaric hordes devoted to political correctness.

"Things were no better when I attended the MLA's 1986 con-vention. The program was . . . bewildering: hundreds upon hun-dreds of conferences devoted to such special themes as 'Eddie and May's Old Man: Theatricality in Sam Shepard's *Fool for Love,*' 'Hannah Cooks the Turkey: Woody Allen's Accommodations of Postmodern Irony,' 'The Repressions of Psychoanalysis: Lesbians, Mothers, and Others in Literature and Theory,' and many, many more." Missing from this book, which was published as part of a se-ries of anti-multicultural books by Whittle Direct Books, was any record of the number of conferences devoted to "traditional" litera-ture at this, or other, MLA conventions.

I am a member of the association and I've inspected literature distributed by the MLA. It is almost worshipful in its attitude to-ward the Western canon.

Has Academia been taken over by radicals with tenure? I un-dertook the task of going to San Diego and attending a Modern Language Association meeting, where I was able to interview those who are usually left out of the discussion when the topic of the po-litical atmosphere on campus is discussed. They are rarely invited to appear on talk shows, which compete with each other in creat-ing excitement among their listeners by promoting an image of American campuses overrun by black malcontents. The resulting hysteria has created an atmosphere in which black students at Penn. State, Brown, and other campuses have been threatened. I found such opinion to be exaggerated, and another example of the media and neoconservative commentators joining in on a propa-ganda attack against African-Americans.

Most of those who write about the experiences of blacks and Hispanics are middle-aged whites like Stephan and Abigail Thern-strom on the right and Jonathan Kozol on the left. (Though the Thernstroms arguments about affirmative action at the University of California at Berkeley were found to be flawed by Vice Chancellor for Undergraduate Affairs, Genaro M. Padilla, in an April 13, 2002, letter to the *Wall Street Journal*, the Thernstroms continue to make good copy, while Padilla is ignored. They appeal to the media's right-wing demographics.) I asked my daughter Tennessee Reed to write a book about her experiences as a black student who is also disabled. I wanted to get the opinions of a person who was connected to the subject, empirically, instead of one who relies on graphs and footnotes. After reading her book, *Spell Albuquerque: L.D. and Mixed in Color-Blind America* (in manuscript), I decided that charter schools would be the best way to educate Hispanics and blacks. Not the charter schools supported by the G.O.P., whose idea of an educator is cultural warrior Lynne Cheney, but charter schools that would prepare students to live in a global neighborhood, schools where they won't be abused by white teachers who refer to them as "animals" and make other insensitive remarks and gestures that damage their self-esteem during the early crucial period of their lives.

As part of AmeriCorps, my daughter worked as a tutor in the classroom of an Oakland ghetto school alongside a white teacher. Seeing that my daughter was more successful in getting black children interested in learning, the white teacher, who had treated the children harshly, under the banner of "tough love," requested that my daughter be transferred to another site. She told the students whose confidence my daughter had gained that Tennessee had "quit." We insisted that Tennessee be given an opportunity to address the students so that they wouldn't think that here was another adult who'd disappointed them. When she explained to the students why she was leaving, the students applauded her and thanked her for helping them, as their other teacher stood by, red-faced. This is not to indict all white teachers, some of whom are dedicated to improving the skills of black students, but in the case of others, there ought to be a law preventing them from coming within a mile of a black student. Moreover, some black teachers can be just as bad. Tennessee reported a black teacher whose behavior was even more abusive than the white teacher's. She kept referring to her students as "Mfs" and threatening them with weapons.

After the events of September 11, 2001, I am more convinced than ever that such a global education is required, not only for black students, but for white, brown, red, and yellow students as well. The destruction of the World Trade Center and a segment of the Pentagon not only ended our political isolation but undercut the theory held by American educators that a superficial knowledge of the traditions of a handful of European countries makes a person smart. Tennessee doesn't see any takeover of American campuses by black students. In fact, there are few black students on the UC–Berkeley campus, from which she graduated on May 17, 2001, due to Proposition 209, which ended gender and racial affirmative action. Tennessee found herself in classrooms where she was the lone African-American student. Only 126 black students were admitted to the University of California at Berkeley last fall.

Tennessee reports that white students in classes she attended at Laney Community College and Berkeley, and even some Asian-American students, did not hesitate, without fear of debate or reprisal, to make racist statements about African-Americans. Not only do some professors fail to correct them, but they often lead the racist attacks. She also reports that blacks and Hispanics complain that they receive lower grades than white students even though their work might have as much merit or might even be of a higher quality. This complaint might be dismissed by the Fox types as P.C., but it's certainly something that should be looked into. She and other black students have sat in classes where professors supported arguments about black inferiority. Some professors have defended the Klan. One professor showed Tarzan movies and led the white and Asian-American students in laughter at the scenes that showed Africans as buffoons. Political correctness on campus? My daughter and other black and Hispanic students haven't found any, nor have the black professors whom I interviewed at the MLA convention in San Diego.

Tennessee and other black students appreciated a true historian, Professor Leon Litwack. She said that his lectures about the lice infesting the underside of American history often left some of his white students confused, disturbed, and angry. White students need to be exposed to more professors like Litwack (*Trouble in Mind*), someone who will tell them the truth, no matter how painful that might be. Then, when blacks complain about being disenfranchised, they won't be dismissed as engaging in victimization, the viewpoint of Shelby Steele, writing in the *International Herald Tribune* about black protests of election violations in Florida. They would know that black disenfranchisement is as much a part of a historical pattern as lynching carried out after a white woman's false accusation of rape.

Though the Brownmiller feminists tried to re-lynch Emmett Till, believing that white women who accuse black men of rape are always telling the truth, Barry Sheck, using DNA evidence, said on Terry Gross's National Public Radio show that 50 percent of the black men who've been accused of raping white women were innocent. "Regardless of what Eldridge Cleaver said," he added. Gross, whose program is black-male-bashing central, and who frequently associates black men with the mistreatment of women, seemed stunned by statement. Did this change her thinking? No. In a later show, she tried to goad a South African white woman into saying that, in South Africa, rape was interracial, instead of intraracial. To the woman's credit, she didn't go along with Gross. Though she had been raped by a black man, she said that white men in South Africa were also guilty of rape.

The false accusation by a white woman of rape, which has led to black men being lynched, black neighborhoods being bombed, and blacks massacred, touched the family of writer and arts impresario Quincy Troupe. His son, Quincy Brandon Troupe, was accused of rape and Quincy Troupe had to face the taunts of those addicted to the suburban myth that most rapes are interracial. Like the black man who was supposed to have raped a white woman in

1921, a rumor that led to the massacre of over 300 people in Tulsa, Oklahoma, his son was exonerated. But this false charge was one of the reasons why Troupe and Margaret Porter moved to La Jolla, California, from their apartment in Harlem, which had become a salon for a number of writers: black, Hispanic, and white. La Jolla, an upscale white community, was uncharted territory. None of us knew what was in store for them. John A. Williams, the novelist, was afraid that the Troupes would suffer a racist reception. I was present when John expressed his concern. Quincy answered with a stoical smile, "There are crackers everywhere."

Quincy and Margaret have done well in La Jolla. He has brought the stars of the literary world for performances at the San Diego Museum and the University of California at San Diego, where he teaches. He has also followed up his book, *Miles: The Autobiography*, one of the most important books of jazz since the term was first used at the turn of the last century, with a book entitled *Miles and Me*. The invasion of La Jolla by this cultural general hasn't been without incident. Tom Metzger, leader of a branch of American Nazis, sought a confrontation with Quincy Troupe, backstage at the San Diego Museum. Racist leaflets were left on the lawn in front of the Troupe house. Quincy Troupe has achieved international recognition as a result of his appearing on the Bill Moyers show and the success of his two books about Miles Davis, a man who helped change modern music, who for many years strove for perfection and who was a prime example of someone devoted to the work ethic, yet was dismissed by the *Times* as a "pimp."

Troupe, the arts impresario, is not bereft of outlets. Others must make their witness in virtual silence. Both black men and women are singled out for police harassment daily, and if the police put whites under as much surveillance as they do blacks, there would probably be five times as many inmates in the nation's jails than there are now.

When it comes to the law enforcement, the police can't distinguish between a black feminist and a black misogynist. In the

1930s, Jewish women in Germany made an alliance with Aryan feminists and critiqued the Jewish patriarchy, but when the government went right, real right, they were abandoned by their Aryan allies. Jewish feminists and Jewish patriarchs were sent to the camps on the same trains. Maybe it won't come to that in this country for black men and women, but always, in the back of the mind of every black person, is the example of what happened to Native Americans, who were sent to camps on trains, and the Japanese-Americans who suffered the same fate. Blacks are always looking over their shoulders at this history. The dilemma faced by minority feminists is that their criticisms of minority men will provide ammunition for their enemies. For African-Americans every day is a day at the front. And in the most dangerous situations, class and gender differences between them dissolve. After an encounter with a policeman who didn't know that he was a Pulitzer Prize winner, James Allan McPherson found that out. Until then, he had been advocating an Ellisonian transracialism (a utopian goal that we'd all embrace), but he realized that a policeman will de-universalize you, on behalf of white society, or go upside your particular head. After this pronouncement, and his remark that he preferred Japanese to American society, critics who had once praised McPherson's Ellisonian stance scolded him in print.

Whether one is a marginal underclass person residing in the inner city, or whether one is a world-famous celebrity like Sonny Rollins, every black man has to pass the inspection of the white patrollers as he maneuvers through American society. When the white patrollers are not doing it, they assign the task to near-whites. When I travel to Piedmont, an wealthy district in Oakland, to take my Japanese lessons, it's the Mexican workers who give me the once-over.

Police incidents led to the riots of the 1960s, and still lead to riots. Cities across the nation lose millions of dollars each year as the result of police brutality suits, yet the white population, when polled, doesn't see police brutality as a problem. We don't see no

xxx   **Another Day at the Front**

problem. What's the problem? What? Black men continue to be shot down in the streets by the police and, for these murders, the police receive a slap on the wrist, or even a promotion. One of the men who killed Amadou Diallo is set to get a swell job in the fire department, sort of like a reward.

The police are the patrollers of the twenty-first century and their role hasn't changed.

But no matter the difficulty faced by contemporary black men, even those who are famous and honored, none has had to confront the kind of hostility faced by Booker T. Washington and his contemporaries. One of the favorite pastimes for some Southern whites, in those days, was hunting black men and lynching them.

I recently made some favorable remarks about Booker T. Washington, based upon research I'd conducted at the Washington archives at Hampton University. When I presented this information in Seattle, the Southern members of the audience gave me a warm response. A black mainstream journalist, however, one of the few remaining in the profession, scolded me. (He's mainstream now but in the 1930s he was a left-wing Chicago radical.) For him, Booker T. Washington was an "Uncle Tom." This is a common characterization of this man by critics, mostly intellectuals in the North, who practice their militancy on campuses, sometimes located in communities where blacks are rare. At the invitation of a writer and educator, Haki Madhubuti, I defended Washington before an audience of writers, scholars, and intellectuals. The reception was cool but polite. Perhaps I should have added a personal anecdote as to why, regardless of his faults, Booker T. Washington will always be honored in my household. When my natural father, a college graduate, refused any responsibility for my support, my mother was left in poverty. She not only had an infant to take care of, but a mother who was afflicted with schizophrenia. One of the brightest students in her high school, she could have completed college without difficulty. But in those days, there were very few options for a single mother. When she went to Buffalo, New York, to seek a better living, I was left, for a period of time, with my grandmother's brother, a colorful character and ragtime piano player, known throughout Chattanooga, Tennessee, affectionately, as "Chick." His wife was an Indian-looking woman named Lou.

His name was Emmett Coleman (which a careless scholar, writing about me in Gale Research's *Contemporary Authors*, said was my given name and that I'd changed it to Ishmael. He should take this up with my mother, who named me Ishmael). His career as a worker in the pipes work, located at the bottom of the hill upon which his future home would stand, was short-lived. He was found asleep on the job one day and was fired. He always delighted in retelling what his foreman said when he found him asleep. He said, don't wake him. As long as he is asleep, he has a job. Obviously, my uncle, an early role model, was not cut out for the kind of grunt work to which most of the black men of his day were consigned. He learned tailoring from my mother's cousin, Ishmael Hubbard, my namesake. As a result, my uncle was able to go to his job at Miller Brother's department store clean. Shoes shined, well-tailored suits, and sometimes wearing a rakish straw hat. Ishmael Hubbard learned his craft at Tuskegee Institute. In a sense, Booker T. Washington was responsible for there being food on our table: chicken, rice, pinto beans, cornbread, and bread pudding on Sundays.

Thousands of Southern blacks could make the same claim. While Booker T. Washington sought to improve the condition of his fellow blacks, he was opposed, not only by Northern elitists like W. E. B. DuBois, but by a stubborn resistance, whose nature was set by John C. Calhoun, another white ethnic. Calhoun held blacks in the same regard that the British held his Scots-Irish ancestors. This fierce resistance convinced Booker T. Washington that the majority of whites would never accept integration. He was right!

John C. Calhoun is not the only descendant of those whom Fox Butterfield, writing in the *New York Times*, refers to as "white savages" to receive a whiteness upgrade by denigrating blacks. In a speech before the Irish Colloquium at the University of California at Davis and in an article published in Rabbi Michael Lerner's *Tikkun*, I referred to those who've forgotten where they came from as the Ersatz.

A few weeks later, in a speech before the National Council of Teachers of English, I discussed the effect on other youth of blaming everything on blacks, a trend that has made policy wonks and op-ed writers and columnists gobs of money and promoted the brand-name news operations and talk shows, but has been detrimental to the nation's youth. Toni Morrison, Nobel laureate, was right to call the media "quisling" in a 2001 commencement speech. They cover up white pathology, the crimes of the corporations, and blame blacks for racism. They are the ones who made affirmative action a "black preference" program, following the cynical tactic of their right-wing owners. Since I am not bereft of outlets, I have been able to challenge some of the libeling of African-Americans, the men especially, by the media. This has brought me into conflict with some of those whose products I've criticized. When David Simon, author of *Homicide*, was on tour for his book *The Corner*, I called in to KPFA radio, on which he was being interviewed, to protest his requiring a young black teenager to accompany him on his book tour. I likened it to Buffalo Bill touring with real live Indians. The teenager seemed to be on board to give Simon's *The Corner*, all about black people doing and selling drugs, a stamp of authenticity. Later, Simon appeared on Amy Goodman's show, *Democracy Now*, and had some chuckles at the young man's expense as he recounted some anecdotes about his lifestyle. Simon said that I was being "defensive," which I interpreted to mean that I was unhappy about the images of black people he'd presented. He also said that the kind of underclass blacks that he presented were rarely shown in the media, which favor middle-class blacks. (He said this. No lie.) He, like the police booster Richard Price, author of *Clockers*, praised the police. Simon's view of the Baltimore police is disputed by the black author of *Klandestine*, who said that some of them are members of the Klan. Amy Alexander said that she witnessed a clash that Simon had with a white reporter who was going to do a ghetto story. Simon felt that the reporter was invading his turf.

I had written a play about the drug trade, *Hubba City*. It didn't merely cover the street corner end, but included other classes and ethnic groups in on this multibillion dollar business, without which, Michael Levine, an author and former Drug Enforcement Agency agent, has said, the Western economy would collapse. I published an essay in the *Washington Post* about this play, in which some of the characters referred to government involvement in drug sales. It was written before Gary Webb, then a reporter for the *San Jose Mercury News*, exposed these operations.

Home Box Office produced a series based upon *The Corner*, and it was awarded an Emmy. Again, Simon used a black, this time a black actor, Charles Dutton, to finesse his project for the public. (Jon Entine and John Hoberman, who have this thing about black athletes, also toss black bodies into the path of their critics.) The actor made the acceptance speech, while Simon stood behind him. Simon told a *New York Times* reporter that I was against his doing this piece of work, which I considered sleazy, because he was a white man! Talk about the race card. I told the reporter that I was opposed to the piece because it was a cliché. It would be like my doing a series on Jewish life and featuring Inside Traders or doing one on Irish-American life and showing a bunch of drunks, or representing Italian-American life with the Sopranos. My response to Simon was never printed in the *Times*. The reason is, I suspect, that the *Times* covers the same side of the Corner as Simon. Do you think that HBO would permit Simon to do a series about Citibank's involvement in the drug trade? It gets worse. One of Simon's collaborators, George P. Pelecanos, was the guest on a book show on KPFA. He was pushing his crime novel *Hell To Pay* and during the interview, launched into a tirade about blacks in Washington, D.C., Marion Barry, whom he described as having a "pathological" need for publicity, and black men who have no responsibility toward their children, which, in a country where one

Instead of expressing remorse to the black employees who were insulted by this program, the arrogant types who run NPR, including Nina Totenberg, who set up Anita Hill and praised *The Bell Curve,* did a sequel to "Ghetto Life 101."

When I sent an e-mail complaining about what I called "audio child molestation," NPR got its token Hispanic, Ray Suarez, to reply to me. Suarez said that these child journalists were superior to Bryant Gumbel and Ed Bradley, whom he described as "rich, showcase blacks." Showcase? Ray Suarez is the kind of malleable conservative Hispanic with whom the people at PBS and NPR are comfortable. (Another one is Rick Sanchez, MSNBC's right-wing Cuban-American anchorman.) During a program in which he interviewed some Hispanic intellectuals, he bragged, "I didn't need Chicano studies when I went to college." Now I can understand an uninformed athlete like Kobe Bryant doing an ad for a despicable bigot, Don Imus, whose hateful comments about blacks can be found at www.tompaine.com, but black intellectuals sometimes demonstrate that they are just as gullible. Cornel West and Henry Louis Gates Jr. were so thrilled to get on NPR that they overpraised Suarez and one of them called him "a national treasure."

Disclaimer. NPR gave me a commentary about the time that President Bush the first was taking office, but they let me go after I submitted a commentary predicting that the Willie Horton ads, in which the image of a black rapist was used to scare whites into voting for Bush, would backfire on Bush and Lee Atwater, who, with Roger Ailes, the current president of Fox TV, designed the ads. I've also had a run-in with PBS when I accused them of using Nazi-like images to smear all black youth in a Roger Rosenblatt essay about the Central Park rape of a stockbroker.* The producer of the essay requested that my publisher make me apologize, like the owner of one plantation requesting that the owner of another discipline an

---

*Sept. 4, Barry Sheck, appearing on CNN said that new DNA evidence exonerates the convicted youth. He said that they confessed to the crime because detectives said they could go home if they did so.

unruly slave. I refused and my editor agreed with me about the essay after I mailed him a videotape.

My relations with Pacifica have been quite good. I had a show on KPFA once and discontinued the show only because I was very busy at the time. Whenever I want to express an opinion or promote a book or play, I can always gain access to KPFA's airwaves. I have disagreements with some of the programming. I think that white feminists, who have a lot of power at the station, obey a double standard for black and white men. (So do white and black feminists at the *New York Times, The Nation,* Salon.com, the *Village Voice,* and, of course, NPR.) They'll do a show criticizing Mike Tyson, but I doubt that in light of Tatum O'Neal's revelations about her brutalization at the hands of John McEnroe, the feminists there will do a show about it. I sent an e-mail to the National Organization for Women asking whether the group was going to picket John McEnroe, as it did Mike Tyson. NOW didn't respond. We have two women-batterers doing sports for NBC, McEnroe and Marv Albert. Why don't the networks just go ahead and give O.J. his old job back?

I thought that Pacifica's coverage of the Los Angeles riots, which resulted from the acquittal of the police who brutalized Rodney King, was superior to that of the corporate media, which blamed the whole thing on black gangs. Pacifica did mention that the typical rioter was Hispanic. (Yet, C-Span's *Washington Journal* posed the topic, "Have the L.A. riots changed your mind about race?" Since Hispanic is a linguistic category, perhaps the topic should have been put, "Did the L.A. riots change your mind about language?") But like the corporate media, Pacifica presented Korean store owners as victims and made no mention of the fact that black business owners lost millions of dollars as well. When it comes to protecting the image of whites, Pacifica is part of the conspiracy of silence.* No mention was made of the white rioters. Mayor Tom Bradley said that it was whites who burned down Korean stores in Korea Town. Depsite these criticisms, I still rely

---

*Fifteen percent of those arrested during the L.A. riots were white.

upon Pacifica for the news and information missing from corporate media and from NPR and PBS, which have been scared into a sort of tepid cowardly middle by the right. And so, when Pacifica announced that it was going to devote a whole day of programming to Juneteenth, an important date for Black Americans, marking the year when Texas blacks heard about the Emancipation, I was interested. I tuned into Amy Goodman's Pacifica show "Democracy Now," and what did I get? Some black kids talking about their life on the streets, selling crack, and so on. And who was the producer of this thing called "Portraits of Youth"? David Isay.

On July 26, 2002, the reporters for "Ghetto Life 101," now adults, appeared on NPR to market a documentary of their show that was being produced by Showtime. It's appropriate that this black-exploitation documentary be produced by a cable channel with that name. Even thought Susan Stamberg, the host, didn't invite the show's black critics to appear with the reporters, one of the reporters acknowledged that they had received criticism from some of the residents who'd appeared on "Ghetto Life 101." One of the reporters justified the project on the basis that it had told the "truth." Well, a number of ethnic groups, including Stanberg's, have "truths" that ought to be exposed. These young men must ask themselves, why is it only the "truths" about one aspect of African-American culture that are always being exposed, and do outfits like Showtime and Home Box Office broadcast such "truths" from the feeling of compassion or as tax write-offs, or to lure subscribers who get turned on by 'hood culture? Moreover, did the two reporters, who've garnered Peabodys and other awards, turn their profits over to the residents of the projects from which they and their producers derived their material? These young men have been associated with NPR since the age of twelve, and they still don't get it.

Though David Simon, Mickey Kaus, David Isay, and Richard Price will continue to earn money by taking out after the moral lapses of people in the inner city or downing welfare recipients, apparently, the drug crisis has become so bad among whites that even the media, which up to now has regarded drugs as a black problem, have had to take notice. The excuses we got in the 1990s from the media bosses was that the image of blacks goes along with drugs because blacks deal out in the open. Not according to Joseph Jett, author of *Black and White on Wall Street*. He said that the white traders on Wall Street did coke, openly, without anybody swooping down on them and placing them before a judge to be given a mandatory minimum sentence of five to twenty years.

And so when I saw *Traffic*, the movie, and the white fraternity boy told off the Mike Douglas character in that scene where they go to a black ghetto to retrieve Douglas's addicted daughter, I applauded. The Douglas character, all high and mighty, scolds his daughter's boyfriend "for bringing my daughter into a neighborhood like this." The young man tells him that there are hundreds of thousands of white kids going into neighborhoods like this. I know that white kids have been coming into my Oakland inner-city neighborhood for years seeking drugs. The only problem with this film, which showed how drugs have affected white youth, was that the dealers were black. There's enough evidence to show that white adults are doing drugs too. The *Philadelphia Inquirer* said that heroin abuse in the suburbs was "skyrocketing," but this story was almost hidden by the *New York Times*, which often exhibits display photos of blacks smoking dope.

Also, as a former cabinet member, Joseph Califano had to remind people, appearing on a Chris Matthews show in January 2001, that people buy drugs from people of their own background. White kids buy drugs from their school mates, he said. MSNBC, the cable network on which he said this, did a feature on drugs about the same time, but here again the drug addicts were white and the dealers black. Once in a while you get a rare film with white dealers, like *The Sleeper*, or *Blow*, whose message was that the cocaine epidemic began not in the Chicago projects haunted by filmmakers with foundation and CPB grants, but in Hollywood. In both films, all of the dealers were white.

Nevertheless, *Traffic* and the MSNBC report were a far cry from *The Corner*, which, once again portrayed blacks as the only ones hooked on addiction in the nation that drug lord Carlos Lehder called "A Nation of Junkies." We are a pig-out nation that dumps its slops on the entity known as the black community. Every nation, it seems, has a place where it relieves itself. In the United States blacks are that place. You realize the damage when you tune into white callers venting on the talk shows. I experience the damage when I try to educate my white students, whose ideas about race are no different from those callers.

Kweisi Mfume, N.A.A.C.P. head, addressing a convention of broadcasters, said that the Sunday news shows on which unanswered generalizations are made, weekly, about African-American issues may not have a large viewing audience, but they influence what he refers to as " the psychological demographics," that is opinion and policymakers. The bashing of minorities by Tim Russert is more benign that that of MSNBC's Don Imus, who got into trouble with the National Association of Black Journalists, during the week of July 17, 2002, for referring to basketball star Allen Iverson's wife as a "naked 'ho" and his mother as a "crack 'ho." Neither Russert nor his mentor, Senator Daniel Moynihan, will acknowledge the drastic reduction of out-of-wedlock births among black women. Their refusal to acknowledge these statistics can be seen as part of a propaganda effort aimed at furthering white resentment against blacks. To oppose this continued slander is to be engaged in a daily battle. I believe that the white right and their African-American mind doubles consider this to be the case. Maybe that's why it's not surprising that the professional critics of blacks use the language of war. John McWorther talks of black Americans' "self sabotage." Richard Bernstein talks about white culture being at war and recommends that his side "man the battlements." (I wonder whether the white youngsters who threatened Dale Allender, an executive with the National Council of Teachers of English, for teaching a multicultural course had gotten their charge from Bernstein.)

People say, well, why are you spending time writing these hard-hitting essays, like someone who stays in the gym all day, punching bags. Get a life, why don't you? they ask. Why are you wasting time with these confrontational in-your-face rants, when you could be writing novels and poetry at that house you rent in Hawaii? On the ocean. I still write novels and poetry, but I'll tell you why I write essays that are direct and controversial to some, so much so that people threaten me with violence. Others, like Jon Entine, get their feelings hurt when I compare their theories about blacks with those of fascists. In a self-pitying, whining manner he finally confessed to me that his book about black athletes having a genetic edge in sports was written to make money. "I did it to put food on the table," he said, during a Perry Mason moment on the phone with me. In a panel held in Harlem, in an obvious reply to Entine, the late Stephen Jay Gould denied the existence of a "speed gene" and a Kenyan runner who shared the panel with him said that Kenyan runners achieve their excellence through hard work, and though Entine attempts to commercialize his work with a brazen website that promotes his theory as some sort of new product, racist sports writers have always argued that black athletes excel because of animal-like endowments. They said it about Joe Louis whom they pretended to adore. They say it now about the Williams sisters.

Those who maintain that people are "afraid to talk" about blacks are out of touch with reality. I watch television and read newspapers, and all we get, daily, are people who aren't afraid to discuss blacks in the most hurtful way, meant to insult and humiliate. When they aren't ragging black Americans, they rag Africans.

More black, Latino, and Asian-American journalists are leaving mainstream journalism, an outfit so insensitive that at the convention of the American Society of Newspaper Editors, delegates laughed at demeaning jokes about Chinese-Americans. The American Society of Newspaper Editors has admitted that newspapers have failed to meet the challenge, made by the late Robert Maynard, publisher of the *Oakland Tribune*, that newsrooms diversify by the year 2000. The National Press Club must not know this, because the club gave an award to a writer, William McGowan, au-

thor of *Coloring the News,* who attributes what little diversity that
has occurred in the newsrooms to—P.C.! According to *USA Today,*
Richard Prince, a *Washington Post* editor and member of the National Association of Black Journalists, said the book is full of "half-
truths, spin and inaccuracies and it not worthy of an award from a
journalistic organization!" And by the way, since individuals and institutions are apologizing for wrongs inflicted upon others,
shouldn't the American Society of Newspaper Editors apologize to
African-Americans, Asian-Americans, and indigenous people (Native Americans and Hispanics) for the role of newspapers in inciting mob violence against these groups in the past?

Barbara Reynolds said that she was fired from *USA Today* because her columns didn't appeal to their demographics of angry
white males. The late Carl Rowan said that he lost his job as a
syndicated columnist because he was " too old and too bold." A
black publisher of the *San Jose Mercury News* quit his job because they were trying to hold him to a bottom-line mentality.
Courageous journalists like George Curry and Tavis Smiley lost
their jobs at *Encore* magazine and BET because their employers
felt that they were coming on too strong. In an article entitled
"Mainstream Newspapers Fade to White," a black journalist, Lee
Hubbard, noted a decline in the number of black journalists in
newsrooms, a situation that's gotten worse since the publication
of my book *Airing Dirty Laundry.* Symptomatic of the ethnic
cleansing occurring in newsrooms is the situation at the *Daily
News* in New York.

"In January 1993, upon buying the *News,* Mort Zuckerman
fired about 180 staffers, including some nine black editorial employees," according to the *Village Voice.*

"They fired all of the African American men on the reporting
staff."

The only black opinion makers with any visibility are those who
serve as mind doubles for their neoconservative or right-wing
bosses, even though a recent survey, cited by a *USA Today* colum-

nist, showed very little support for black conservatives among the black population.

As long as I have a platform, I think that I have an opportunity to combat the slander and libel aimed at blacks as a group. Does this sound too black? Well, a racist society will often force you to engage in "essentialism," from time to time. I would prefer living as a world person on a planet that accepts differences instead of on one that is dull and monochromatic. But a funny thing happened to me while enroute to this perfect world. I was fined for living while black. Being "universal" is difficult in a country where African-Americans are defined by the police, by the red-liners, by the racial and retail profilers, by the rude treatment in everyday life by people who are prejudiced. (Next time I'm subjected to racial and retail profiling, I'll remind the policeman, or the department store security guard, that race is a social construct.) And though I own my Native American and European-American heritage, my nerves must be black, because I get a visceral reaction when I feel that blacks, as a group, are treated unfairly.

Like the time I was driving to University of California at Davis to meet with my fellow members of the Irish diaspora with the radio turned to a public radio show called *Connections*. The show that day was about AIDS and the black community's alleged silence about it. I was furious, not because I don't believe that AIDS is a grave crisis in the black community or because I know that other ethnic groups are secretive about AIDS or because I'm aware that many institutions in the black community, including churches, are mobilizing African-Americans in the fight against AIDS, but because I know that public radio seeks to boost its ratings by doing shows that embarrass blacks and entertain whites. In this respect, public radio is no different from the corporate media. The producers' motives for doing this show were lousy. (During the week of May 23, a public-radio moderator and a woman who had written the kind of book about Africa that's popular these days, exempting white colonialism or neocolonialism from any responsibility for the turmoil taking place in some countries, shared some laughs. Neither the host nor the author speculated about what the history of post-colonial Africa might have been had not certain "independent" nations been caught in a struggle between the United States and the former Soviet Union, a struggle that led to the overthrow of Kwame Nkrumah, Patrice Lumumba, the ascendancy of Mobutu, and the devastation of countries like Angola, which occurred when Ronald Reagan and his wealthy donors supported "rebel leader" Joseph Savibimbi with millions of dollars. When an African caller reminded them of the millions killed by King Leopold's armies, she said that the numbers were exaggerated.) The yuppie smart aleck full-of-itself voice of the moderator said that this show about AIDS would undoubtedly touch some nerves. We all know whose nerves the show intended to touch. African-American nerves. My nerves.

For some of the white listeners, it was meant to boost their egos, by denigrating others. For me it was psychological nerve gas. And though I had a swell time that day with my Irish-American colleagues, I felt like Countee Cullen, the African-American poet. All he could remember from his trip to Baltimore was being called a nigger. All I could remember from that day was the false accusation that black churches, because of their homophobia, have done nothing to fight AIDS. This was propaganda pure and simple. But as an African-American male, I'm used to it. Here's the paradox. I live in a country that's been good to me but is also at war with me. My antecedents can say the same. Booker T. Washington and W. E. B. DuBois had their days at the front. So did Harriet Tubman and Sojourner Truth. Even someone as gentle as Countee Cullen had his days at the front. My generation continues to have its hit-and-run encounters with white supremacy. The generation to which Paul Beatty, Anthony Grooms, and Colson Whitehead belong is having theirs.

The essays in this book will probably draw the same response as my previous ones. Some will agree with the arguments put forth here, others will disagree. Some of these disagreements will become vehement. I welcome this.

CHAPTER 1

The Sermons That Clinton Should Give

WHEN PRESIDENT CLINTON SPEAKS AT BLACK AND LATINO churches about escalating violence in their communities, on the face of it, this effort to reach out would seem to be a compassionate gesture. I voted for Clinton because I believed that he was capable of compassion. But when I read that Stanley Greenberg, Clinton's pollster, approved of these appearances, I became suspicious.

According to news reports, Greenberg was in part responsible for the episode during the presidential campaign in which Clinton publicly scolded Jesse Jackson for inviting the rap artist Sister Souljah to appear before a meeting of the Rainbow Coalition after she rapped some lyrics that some interpreted as anti-white. Many observers concluded that Clinton's remarks had been deliberately aimed at Reagan Democrats, whom he was wooing by standing up to one of the nation's most prominent black public figures.

Are Clinton's appearances at black and Latino churches part of the same strategy, appealing to conservative voters by blaming blacks and Latinos for America's social problems? He can dispel such doubts about his sincerity by expanding his evangelical crusade.

He can preach to the bankers who probably attend beautiful cathedrals in Washington and New York, because without them those exporting drugs into the United States wouldn't have a place to put their profits. According to the Justice Department, American banks take in $100 billion a year in "dirty money" from the international drug trade. And Clinton could preach to the executives who sell Colombian cartels the chemicals they need to process cocaine. I'm sure that State Department officials attend some of these Washington churches. The president could ask them to search their hearts and meditate about whether their ties to the regimes of drug-producing countries have contributed to the flow of drugs into this country. And Clinton should preach to conservatives in the media (who presumably attend some of these same churches) about hypocrisy. Let's hope those who believe that black dysfunctional families are at the root of all of America's social problems spent time with their own families over the holidays.

The president could then take his mission into the white suburbs. Tell Washington suburbanites to quit going into the city to buy drugs. Representative Walter Fauntroy says 80 percent of those buying drugs on Washington's streets are suburbanites. And if Mr. Clinton is serious about violence, he could preach about spousal abuse in the suburbs.

William Bennett, the former secretary of education, who has been known to say that urban public schools should be abandoned because they are out of control, might be startled to learn that, by most measures, there is little difference between violence in suburban and inner-city schools. He can find the facts in a 1989 Justice Department survey. Clinton can also say a prayer for members of our largest underclass—whites—many of whom live in the suburbs and who are neglected by pundits who often seem to imply that American poverty stems from the life style of blacks.

J. Larry Brown, director of the Center on Hunger, Poverty, and

Nutrition Policy at Tufts University (now at Brandeis University), said about hunger: "It's no longer single mothers, ghettos, minorities and the non-working. . . . There are three times as many poor in the suburbs as there are in the ghettos. The majority of poor people work."

Clinton could establish a commission to study what's ailing teenagers like the two high school honor students in Setauket, Long Island, who sat down on a railroad track in a suicide pact in December. According to school officials, both girls were from stable families. After the president has preached to the well-heeled congregations, he should deliver an address on violence in our country. He should call on everyone to pray about the nationwide problem of depression among children and teenagers. A 1991 federal survey of U.S. high school students found that 27 percent had "thought seriously" about committing suicide in the preceding year; 8 percent had made an attempt. Or Clinton could ask people to pray about the drunk-driving deaths of teenagers. In an article published in the Journal of the American Medical Association, Robert Blum wrote that car accidents account for about 60 percent of all young people's accidents, and more than half of those can be attributed to drunk driving.

Clinton should also address the proliferation of hate crimes, 60 percent of which are committed by white teenagers. While pictures of black teenagers charged with antisocial behavior are plastered all over the newspapers and TV, the white teenager who was a suspect in a 1993 series of firebombings aimed at Jews, blacks, and Asians in Sacramento received little publicity by comparison. Violence is an American problem. It's not merely a black problem, which you might sometimes think from listening to assorted black-pathology experts whose scapegoating of the single-parent household can't explain the widespread domestic abuse that exists in two-parent households. During his sermon in Memphis in November, Clinton asked what the Rev. Dr. Martin Luther King Jr. would say about these problems if he were alive today. Undoubtedly, King, who was born sixty-five years ago today, would be addressing the problem of violence. But he would be preaching to the entire American family, not just to those members who have been targeted by the media and politicians to bear the blame for America's growing social crisis.

An earlier version of this article
appeared in the *New York Times*,
January 15, 1994

CHAPTER 2

The Battle of San Diego

LAST YEAR, PROFESSOR AND POET LORENZO THOMAS OF THE University of Houston–Downtown informed me that two of my novels, *Mumbo Jumbo* and *Reckless Eyeballing*, would be subjects for a panel during the 110th annual convention of the Modern Language Association, the best known and most powerful of professional teachers organizations. He invited me to attend. As a theory-less writer, who teaches part-time at the University of California at Berkeley, I don't usually feel comfortable at MLA conventions.

MLA gets ridiculed from time to time by those who have an obsession with political correctness, even though the materials that are issued by the association stress traditional literature. It's like the *Newsweek* writer with whom I had an exchange and the *Times* writer who mentioned my book, *Mumbo Jumbo*, both believing that the traditional art museums had yielded to women, multiculturalists, and Hip Hoppers. When these artists are part of the permanent collections of museums, then maybe the traditionalists will have something to worry about. Moreover, though the MLA may give over some panels to gays, women, and minorities, the permanent collection is ancient, white, and male. Here are some of the categories of literature covered by its publications. I downloaded these topics from the MLA website:

MLA Book Categories
New Titles
  African and African American Studies
  American Literature
  Bibliographic and Textual Studies
  British Literature
  Composition Studies
  Computer-Assisted Instruction and Research
  Drama
  Eighteenth Century
  Fifteenth and Sixteenth Centuries
  French Literature
  German Literature
  Language Textbooks
  Linguistics
  Literary Criticism and Theory
  Medieval Studies (before 1400)
  Nineteenth Century
  Nonfictional Prose
  Other Literatures
  Poetry
  Professional Issues
  Prose Fiction
  Publishing and Editing
  Research Guides and Bibliographies
  Seventeenth Century
  Shakespeare
  Spanish, Portuguese, and Latin American Literature
  The Teaching of Language
  The Teaching of Literature
  Twentieth Century
  Women's Studies
  Writing Guides

Last updated 10/16/00. Copyright 2000 The Modern Language Association of America. All rights reserved. Questions or comments to websupport@mla.org.

Even though some nods to multiculturalism exist on this list, there's no sign of a black takeover!

Perhaps sensing my discomfort, some teachers who encounter me at MLA conventions have asked, "What are you doing here?" This time, I told them, I would be writing about the convention. Besides, I'd always wanted to write an article in which I could refer to myself in the third person, as some prizefighters are inclined. An opportunity arose when I covered a panel whose topic was my work.

I hadn't slept much the night before, still in a jet-lagged state after two trips to New York and one to Germany within six weeks, and so when I arrived at the Embassy Suites in San Diego, I thought that I'd rest before attending my first event, a coffee hour held at the HarperCollins booth in the exhibit hall. The desk clerk at the Embassy Suites, however, told me that my room was not available. I was going to have to go over to the MLA exhibit hall wearing my traveling clothes: some brown corduroy pants with a faded, shiny seat and my University of New Mexico at Las Cruces sweatshirt. Later, I was to discover that I had forgotten to pack the rest of my pants and was stuck with the brown cords throughout my stay. I think that I must have stood out among the well-dressed teachers. I had to call ahead to New York to tell Carla, my wife, to pick up some pants so that I wouldn't look unkempt when I attended a performance of my play *The Preacher and the Rapper* on Friday night.

Typical of those handsomely attired convention-goers was Professor Dolan Hubbard of the University of Georgia. Hubbard has an unblemished face with bright, boyish eyes. I fell in next to him. Last time I had seen Hubbard was when the College Language Association, an organization founded by black professors who felt that the MLA didn't meet their needs, invited me to Knoxville, where I delivered a speech about Ku Klux Feminism and its impact upon black male culture.

The point of the speech was that the attitudes of some feminists toward black men are similar to those held by women members of the 1920s Indiana Klan, who supported some of the same issues championed by today's feminists, including fighting spousal abuse and freeing women from their domestic prisons. For example, they insisted that their husbands mind the children while they attended Klan meetings. What they had in common with some of today's feminists was their enmity toward black men. My remarks were based upon a book entitled *Women of the Klan, Racism and Gender in the 1920s*, by Kathleen M. Blee. The speech was so hot that between the hostile glares and murmuring from some of the women feminists and the expressions of approval from other audience members, it was necessary for me to call for calm. Though some conservatives view feminists, gays, and African-Americans as members of a coalition that originated in the 1960s and whose aim is that of corrupting the West, there exists, between these groups, real and growing divisions.

Hubbard said that the majority of those seeking positions teaching African-American studies were white women, and this frustrated black students because they preferred black teachers. He said that many of those applicants were sincere, while others were undoubtedly motivated by careerism and opportunism. His views reflected a debate that was being fought out in the pages of the *Chronicle of Higher Education*, the *People's* magazine of the teaching profession, about whether white feminists had any role in the teaching of black literature. Dolan and I parted when we reached the San Diego Convention Center. I went to the coffee hour that HarperCollins was throwing at Exhibit Hall A to celebrate the *American Literary Mosaic Series*, for which I am general editor. Convention delegates were milling before the HarperCollins display, which was set behind five shiny Victorian urns containing various coffees: Vanilla Nut, Hazelnut, Gourmet French Roast, Amaretto Luxe, and Chocolate Raspberry.

I don't think HarperCollins editor Lisa Moore knew what she was getting into when I answered her invitation to serve as general editor for the four books. To edit the books, I was able to recruit Nicolas Kanellos, Shawn Wong, Gerald Vizenor, and Al Young. Nicolas Kanellos is a professor at the University of Texas at Houston and director of Arte Publico, the country's largest Hispanic publisher; Shawn Wong is a novelist and professor in Asian-American studies at the University of Washington at Seattle; Gerald Vizenor is a novelist and professor of Native American studies at the University of California at Berkeley; Al Young is a novelist, poet, essayist, sometimes guest professor, and screenwriter. The result was four anthologies covering Asian-American, African-American, Hispanic, and Native-American literature.

This experience has taught me a lot about the politics of the textbook industry, and I'm sure that Lisa Moore at times missed the reasonable and compliant scholars with whom she is accustomed to working, instead of temperamental writers. As I said in the introduction to the four books, Nicolas Kanellos, Al Young, Gerald Vizenor, and Shawn Wong are not only teachers and writers, but among the pioneers of their respective literatures. So when an upstart editorial assistant tried to give Kanellos some advice about the editing of his volume of Hispanic literature, Kanellos fired back that telling him about Hispanic literature was like telling Jimmy Carter about peanuts.

Gerald Vizenor insisted that the contributors to his textbooks be Native American, not translators or tourists. Shawn Wong, editor of the Asian-American volume, is a key figures in a bitter feud in the Asian-American literary community pitting him and Frank Chin against feminist supporters of Maxine Hong Kingston, who has been accused of turning ancient Chinese texts into feminist tracts in her novels and nonfictional works. Her most famous work is an "autobiography," *The Woman Warrior*. Wong, at first, balked at including the work of those who were on the other side of the argument, but his good sense and fairness prevailed. He decided to include some of those writers, but to make his views known about their work in his introduction.

Another problem we ran into, with members of the editorial staff and with white reviewers and university professors to whom the textbooks were sent for comments, was the reviewers' insistence that their favorite ethnic writers be included in the volumes, no matter how much these writers might be prized because their views accommodate those of the establishment, or no matter how despised they might be in their communities.

In addition to serving as general editor for these textbooks, I am editing a 1,000-page textbook entitled *Literature Across America, from Totem to Rap.* The average textbook is required to duplicate 60 to 80 percent of the material found in other textbooks. This explains why textbooks of literature read alike and why it's so difficult to change them so that today's students may read not only writings from the past, but become acquainted with the best of today's writing. I also discovered why they're devoted to tradition. There is nothing wrong with traditionalism, except instead of being multi-traditional, the texts focus upon the writings of the European and European-American elite. We get the unreadable Wallace Stevens, but we don't get the Anglo-Celtic country-western poets of east Tennessee like Dolly Parton, whose work I will include in my textbook, because her work and that of country-western writers like Hank Williams Sr. and Tex Ritter stand up next to the best ballads written. We get modernists like T. S. Eliot and Ezra Pound, but the modernists of Tin Pan Alley who created those venerable American classics, "the standards," are ignored. The four volumes of the *American Literary Mosaic Series* includes works by contemporary Latino, Asian-American, Afro-American, and Native American writers. My textbook, *Literature Across America, from Totem to Rap,* will include blues, rap, gospel, and the disappeared literature of the 1930s worker writers. It will include work from blues artist Bessie Smith; the founder of gospel music, Thomas Dorsey; the young Paul Beatty, who has been called the poet laureate of rap; and one of our neglected Chicago 1930s writers, James T. Farrell.

There's also a notion about American literature that took hold after a 1930s power struggle between middle-class East-of-the-Hudson elitists and Midwest worker writers—a struggle in which the Bohemian New York left prevailed. This is the belief that politics and art don't mix, even though nineteenth-century writers Thoreau, Whitman, and Emerson are very political. (So were Shelley, Blake, Milton, Wordsworth, and Byron.) My textbook will include a section unheard of in textbook publishing: "Politics, Polemics, and Protest."

I hung around the HarperCollins booth for about two hours, leading teachers to the textbook display and urging that they adopt them for their classrooms. At noon I decided to go to a MELUS (Multi-Ethnic Literature of the United States) luncheon, where Barbara Christian, of Berkeley's Afro-American Studies Department, was going to receive an award. But Reginald Martin, a brilliant professor and novelist, wandered by the HarperCollins booth and told me that he was going to present a paper at noon. I decided to cover his paper, then go to see Barbara get her award.

On the way I ran into Ray Federman, super-fiction novelist, American Book Award winner, and professor at the University of Buffalo. He relayed a message from the critic Leslie Fielder, who said he wanted me to come to Buffalo in the spring to attend his retirement ceremonies. He'd requested Camille Paglia, [the late] Allen Ginsberg, and me. I said I'd be glad to do it. Leslie Fiedler was a throwback to the old days when English professors wrote books of criticism that even those outside of the university could understand. His most famous work is *Love and Death in the American Novel*.

I took the elevator to the second floor of the convention center, where the papers were being read. All of the sessions were held in adjoining rooms.

As I entered the session, which had the forbidding title "Composition Pedagogy at Institutions of Higher Learning Underrepresented in Traditional Histories of Rhetoric," Catherine Hobbs Peaden, of the University of Oklahoma, was reading a paper entitled "Invisible Colleges, Domestic Rhetorics, and Colonizing Literacies: Writing the History of Women's Writing Instruction." Most of those in attendance were women. I found those portions of Peaden's paper that I heard to be interesting and, as is always the case with MLA panels, I learned something.

According to Peaden, American women began to become literate after the "Great Awakening" and, through the reading and writing of novels, improved their skills so that by the year 1870, the literary rate among urban men and women was almost equal. Local literary and study clubs, which is what Peaden meant by invisible colleges, or extracurricular institutions also aided in the effort to make American women literate. Other invisible colleges for women were the women's temperance societies, in which women honed their rhetorical skills. Some of the temperance women traveled to the West to teach English to Native American women.

I've been following Reginald Martin's career for more than a decade. His novel *Everybody Knows What Time It Is*, a comic work that received the Deep South Writer's Prize for best novel in 1988, is the ultimate Black Urban Professional satire. Though Martin, lean and serious, was speaking about the past, his paper addressed an issue that explains why the African-American writing of the 1960s (when novelists and poets were striving for a style that reflected that of the masses of African-American people, a revolt that had much to do with the rhetorical style of Malcolm X) was replaced by a wordy, academic, entangled style that began to appear in the middle 1970s. This style is being practiced by those upon whom the literary establishment has bestowed privilege. We went from the prose of the Afro to that of Geri curls. I, for one, find this overarching and precious writing to be embarrassing.

Martin's paper provided part of the answer. He traced this style to the models used by black colleges, the 1611 King James Bible,

Hamlet, Macbeth, and Cicero. The 1611 King James Bible was used by blacks' kidnapers, who insisted that their African captives learn two sections: the Old Testament, which preached punishment of the rebellious slave, and the New Testament, which preached reward for the good slave. This style, which used the passive voice and complex-compound sentences, was copied by black students well into the 1930s. It wasn't until the revolt in black writing of the 1960s that a black writer like Richard Wright was included in the curriculum of historical black colleges, the name given to those colleges founded in the nineteenth century for the purpose of providing ex-African captives with a missionary education. It's significant that those who've been chosen to chastise black male writers, as a way of marketing their books to women's studies departments, write in the pompous Victorian manner of their elitist idol, W. E. B. DuBois.

After Reginald's speech, I went to the MELUS luncheon, which was located a few doors down the hall. I had known Barbara Christian since the 1960s, when she was dating David Henderson, a poet and biographer of Jimi Hendrix. She later moved from New York to California after receiving a Ph.D. from Columbia University. She has worked in Berkeley's African-American Studies Department since the 1970s and received the American Book Award for her book *Black Women Novelists*. Barbara and I have carried on a lively debate for many years about feminist issues.

Barbara Christian said that when she participated in the 1967 takeover of City College in New York, she never knew that she'd be receiving an award during a convention of the MLA. She talked about the rising hostility against blacks as evidenced by the warm media reception to *The Bell Curve* and its linking of race and intelligence, which Barbara saw as a return to the anti-intellectualism of the nineteenth century. She also accused such entertainments as William Buckley Jr.'s *Firing Line* as exaggerating the power of ethnic studies, which she regards as marginal. She sees such entertainments as part of a propaganda assault on multiculturalism and popular culture. Barbara said that the steady castigation waged by the media and the establishment on ethnic studies meant that the ethnic studies were at least successful in one respect, by raising such ferocious opposition.

While the MELUS luncheon drew about sixty people, a panel entitled "Deconstruction in the Age of Culture Studies," held nearby, drew hundreds. I asked Professor Seth A. Streichler if he had learned anything about deconstruction from attending this panel. He said he'd thought he'd learn something but hadn't. A number of professors whom I interviewed said that they couldn't understand some of the papers that were read by their colleagues. Unlike Streichler, they didn't want to be identified by name.

About two, I went over to the panel entitled "Asian-American Literature Twenty-Five Years After the Third World Strike." Much of the discussion centered around the dispute between Maxine Hong Kingston, her yellow feminist supporters, and Frank Chin, Shawn Wong, Lawson Inada, and Jeffery Chan, editors of the landmark and controversial volume *The Big Aiiieeeee!*

The first speaker was Rajini Srikanth of Tufts University. She said that Southwest Asian-American writers, those writers who have emigrated or whose parents have emigrated from India, Pakistan, Nepal, Sri Lanka, don't refer to themselves as Asian-American writers and that most of their writing is about subject matter located outside of the United States. She described these writers as not being confined to one place, but multilocal. They refuse to be ghettoized, and they defy categorization. She said that there is no agreement as to what constitutes an Asian-American and that those who are described as such are actually pushing against definitions of themselves.

Her words were different, but they reminded me of one of the classical issues that has concerned black writers, whether one is a writer or a black writer, interesting questions for meetings such as this one and a demonstration of how each immigrant group of writers must test the old questions of American literature.

Next came Shelley Wong, a real feminist bombthrower. She really had it in for Frank Chin and his associates and during her paper referred to him as self-serving, excessive, misogynist, and racist. She described his arguments as specious, strident, phallocentric. She said the debate between Chin and his supporters and Kingston and her feminist supporters was a debate about who shall speak for Asian-Americans, no less. So intense is this debate that it has caused people to have had sleepless nights, said Wong. The argument about the use of the term "autobiography" to market Maxine Hong Kingston's *The Woman Warrior*, a decision made by her publisher, began the dispute.

In an interview I later conducted with Frank Chin, he said that in a private exchange of letters with Kingston, which occurred before the publication of *The Woman Warrior*, he told her that he could back the work if it were termed a work of fiction, but as nonfiction he considered it racist. In her reply, according to Chin, Kingston said that she didn't know that there was a difference between fiction and nonfiction. She also said that blacks had learned that anger doesn't work. Frank said that he took this to mean that Kingston was intent upon catering to the white market instead of telling the truth. Replying to his academic critics, he said that he'd done more to recover the lost reputations of Asian-American writers and to publish contemporary ones than all of his critics combined.

The position of Chin and his allies is that the autobiography is a missionary form used in the United States to woo Asians and others into Christianity and assimilation. During her MLA paper, Wong quoted Chin as saying to Maxine Hong Kingston that he wanted her book to be yellow art by a yellow artist, not an "autobiography" written by a Pocahontas promoted by a white publisher. Pocahontas, Captain John Smith's consort, is, for some male writers, the symbol of the colored woman who collaborates with those opposed to the aspirations of her tribe.

For his opinions about the uses of Chinese texts, Chin has been called a cultural fascist by David Hwang and Amy Tan. Tan performs with a group of authors called the Remainders. (Her part of the show includes whipping some of the male members of the band.) Chin has also been described as the Ayatollah Khomeini of Asian-American literature, and in a review full of ad hominem attacks, the *Village Voice*'s Jeff Yang had some fun at the expense of Chin and his associates by putting a sarcastic twist on the title "The Four Horsemen of Asian-American Literature," a moniker applied to Chin and his associates. Yang said that, for him, Frank represented Death.

The panel and the audience were decidedly pro-Kingston and anti-Chin. The discussion, as well as the question-and-answer period, were dominated by feminists of the sort who seemed to be suffering from gender anxiety. A woman in the audience said that she had interviewed Maxine Hong Kingston and that Kingston was now calling *The Woman Warrior* a mytho-psycho-autobiography. Wong said that Maxine must be sick of people talking about Frank Chin all the time.

When all-out warfare broke out between the Four Horsemen and their followers and Maxine's loyalists in the pages of the San Francisco papers, Ishmael Reed's name was dragged into the fray, as though my criticisms of some of Alice Walker's opinions and projects, specifically Steven Spielberg's adaptation of her novel *The Color Purple*, had ignited a gender battle that spread into other ethnic communities. This would not be the first time that Ishmael Reed and his associates had been accused of inspiring people to mischief. In the 1970s, Al Young and I published articles by Native Americans in *Yardbird Reader* critical of what the authors considered white shamans ripping off their materials, which was termed "cultural imperialism" by Gerald Hobson, a Cherokee writer. The white shamans who were the targets of their articles accused Al Young and Ishmael Reed of putting them up to it. A few years ago Cecil Brown interviewed Toni Morrison for *Mother Jones*. In the interview, Morrison said that the gender fight between black women and black men was being promoted from the outside. The feminist editor of

Mother Jones at the time rejected Morrison's observation. She told Cecil Brown that Ishmael Reed had begun the whole thing.

In 1991, Barbara Smith, writing in *Ms.* magazine, accused Ishmael Reed of being the "ringleader" of black men who were calling black women writers traitors for writing harshly about black men. I never said it. I replied to her comments in a letter to *Ms.*, but the editor, Robin Morgan, formerly with *Rat* magazine and a supporter of the position that male ejaculation is an act of war, refused to print my reply. When Morgan resigned from *Ms.*, she made some angry remarks about Clarence Thomas and Mike Tyson, but said nothing about the attitudes toward women held by her former bosses, the male owners of *Ms.*, Lang Communications. (Incidentally, Maxine Hong Kingston works in the same department as I do at Berkeley. All my encounters with her have been cordial. It was due to the help of her and Isabel Allende that PEN Oakland, of which I am a member, was able to send delegates, including PEN chairperson Floyd Salas, to Spain, where the exclusionist, elitist policies of PEN International were challenged.)

David Lee of UCLA traced the recent history of Asian-American literature, beginning with its nationalist phase in the '60s and '70s. According to him, this phase was followed by the feminist phase, which was ushered in by the success of Kingston's *The Woman Warrior*. Lee said that the present was characterized by heteroglossia and the marketing of multiculturalism. He said that in the 1960s, yellows identified with black power and shared with blacks a repudiation of white power. Yellows were caught in a struggle between whites and blacks. This preoccupation was simplistic, he claimed.

Lee said that 1960s–1970s yellows were part of a postwar, postexclusion generation. They were rebellious, and their racial unity was taken for granted. During this period, Lee said, Asian-Americans went unpublished and were writing in what Lee referred to as "dingy" ethnic enclaves. This writing wasn't supported by the establishment institutions.

The Woman Warrior changed all that. With the publication of this work, Asian-American writing became the vogue. In Lee's words, Asian-American writing ascended from the ghetto into the Book-of-the-Month Club. He argued that the quarrel between Chin and Kingston was not so much an ethnic gender war between nationalists and feminists, but between those with a marginal readership and those with a large readership created partially by white feminist co-optation, which was responsible for the writings by Asian-American women being brought into the academy. In Lee's opinion, we're now at the point where identity is suspect and differences have become a virtue. He called this the capitalistic commodification of multiculturalism. Discussion of differences has replaced a discussion of race, Lee said, as the capitalists strive for a United Nations of the marketplace. Lee said that this was the old divide-and-conquer strategy.

Among Asian-Americans, Lee said, there existed no ethnic consciousness and members of the thirty-nine or so culturally distinct groups do not refer to themselves as Asian-Americans but as Vietnamese, Cambodians, and so forth. He said that unlike the 1960s, a period that emphasized ethnicity, the political struggle was now very localized. I was wondering why none of the supporters, male or female, of Chin and his position were invited to submit papers or why there was no acknowledgment of the Four Horsemen's role in reconstructing a tradition of Asian-American literature. This certainly would have provided balance, not to say a lively discussion. It reminded me of an evangelical meeting where absent sinners were being prayed over so that they might see the errors of their ways.

Like the black scholars who disappear any black writing that doesn't mesh with their notions of what literature should be, Lee failed to mention trailblazing work, published and edited in the '70s by the horsemen, Chin, Wong, Chan, and Inada, *Yardbird Reader #3*, and the first *The Big Aiiieeeee!,* which was published by Howard University Press, a black press. It was as though this literature had been purged. In the hall outside the meeting room, I asked Professor Bobbie To Smith her opinion of the panel. She said that it was typical of the gender fighting that's also happening in African-American and Latino intellectual circles. She objected to the academic jargon, the use of language so as not to communicate, and the posturing. She said that ethnic communities must move beyond the gender battles.

For more than a decade, I had been attending conferences and meetings where feminist issues had swept every other issue off the boards. In fact, one can say that black intellectual life has been stymied by issues of middle-class genderism and by feminist opportunists who, having run out of contemporary black males to tarnish with the career-ending appellation "misogynist," are tarnishing dead ones like Richard Wright, Malcolm X, and Paul Lawrence Dunbar.

An Irish-American progressive who worked for Bobby Kennedy had confided to me his opinion that white feminism had destroyed the left. Black women, according to Professor Shirley Lee, have been accusing white feminists of racism for 100 years, and continue to do so.

The vituperative attacks on Frank Chin by the feminists who attended the Asian-American panel only play into the hands of those who are lurking about looking for evidence of political correctness. Seems that instead of demagoguing down criticisms of intellectuals like Camille Paglia, as Gloria Steinem did on *60 Minutes*, the feminists would welcome Chin's opinions as an opportunity for open debate.

I wandered around the exhibit hall. I ran into Houston Baker Jr., the favorite target of the traditionalists. He invited me to the University of Pennsylvania cash bar, one of many held to recruit new faculty.

By the time I returned to the Embassy Suites, my room was ready and I checked in. After about an hour I headed for the Baker reception. I went to the information booth for assistance and discovered that there were any number of cash bars.

I went to the Marriott and ran into some black scholars, including Barbara Christian (now deceased) and Lorenzo Thomas, who were seated at a table having drinks. A scholar from the Northeast, who didn't want his name to be tied to his comments, was expressing his regrets over his participation in the controversial Whitney Museum's "Black Male: Representations on Masculinity in Contemporary American Art." He is the author of an article that appears in the show's brochure. Though critics at the *Village Voice* and the *New York Times* embraced the show, the response of such publications as the New York *Amsterdam News*, whose subscribers are members of New York's black community, was unfavorable, and some black artists, including Adgar Cowans, a photographer, who produced the stills for such movies as *The Eyes of Laura Mars*, said they were insulted by the show in an interview published in the *New York Times*.

I didn't like the show. I couldn't understand why the Whitney ignored the brilliant black New York painters in favor of works by Mapplethorpe, whose images of black men have been criticized by prominent black gays, including the late Marlon Riggs, the creator of *Tongues Untied*, as racist.

While in New York, I heard African-Americans, men and women, complaining about how those whites who set the trends for African-American culture had put a handful of black feminists and straight-hating gays in charge of New York black culture. I also found myself agreeing with Hilton Kramer who, in the *New York Observer*, charged that the Whitney show was framed by French theory and Warholism. I asked Barbara Christian her opinion of the culture wars and the contention by highly paid public-performance intellectuals that blacks are the ringleaders in an effort to corrupt Western civilization. Barbara said that some whites, through some cognitive glitch, exaggerate the presence of a few blacks in any given institution. "Twenty blacks in a crowd makes the whole crowd seem black" is the way she put it. As for the MLA's going black, she said, "Just look at the program." Though there seemed to be a few concessions made to this multiculturalism that the tabloids and performance intellectuals view as a threat to the survival of the West, most of the panels had to do with the straight, traditional, Eurocentric curriculum. Not only Barbara Christian but others noticed that there were few people of color present at the conference, yet opponents of multiculturalism wrote as though the MLA conferences were the site of war conferences, where blacks and the others convened for the purpose of plotting the demise of the West.

One black scholar told me that the opponents of multiculturalism, were they in England at the time, would have congratulated Thomas Moore for writing in Latin instead of English. Good point. Writer C. J. Wallia, a native of India, and editor of an influential zine devoted to worldwide Indian literature (IndiaStar.com), said that those English writers who are now canonized were not considered worthy to have their works included in the English curricula in a former time and were used only in the colonies. The curriculum in England at the time was Latin and Greek.

Christian, a Ph.D. herself, said that the peak of black Ph.D.s occurred in 1975, and it's been downhill ever since. She said that her chief worry was that ethnic studies, postcolonial studies, and black feminism courses were being conducted without the people who created them, a criticism similar to the one made by Dolan Hubbard, that ethnic studies were now being taken over by whites.

Somebody had told me the night before that there was a lot of interest in a paper that was to be given by Joyce Ann Joyce, author of *Warriors, Conjurers and Priests: Defining African-Centered Literary Criticism*, but it wasn't until I reached the hall on Thursday and read the program that I realized that the subject of her talk was my work. First, I had breakfast with Lisa Moore, my HarperCollins editor. We shared a table with Professor Ralph Rader, chairperson of the Berkeley English Department. He was holed up in the Embassy Suites recruiting young faculty. He told me that the younger scholars seemed to be more interested in theory than in how theory was applied.

Occasionally there is a challenge to New York's control over African-American culture. In the 1930s, the Midwest worker writers referred to New York as "East of the Hudson," as though this were a demonic area. The Midwesterners, led by Jack Conroy, author of *The Disinherited*, criticized what they considered bourgeois modernism of the New York writers, bohemians, and intellectuals who were alienated from the common people. Jack Conroy and his group lost out to the Francophilic modernists after a power struggle in which *Partisan Review* prevailed over the Midwest radicals' publication, *The Anvil*.

Partisan Review published James Baldwin's famous attack on Richard Wright, "Everybody's Protest Novel." Richard Wright had been associated with the Conroy group.

In the 1960s, *Black World*, edited by Hoyt Fuller and published in Chicago by Johnson Publications, publishers of *Ebony*, challenged the New York literary establishment's control over the trends in African-American culture and thought and formed a literary circle that included Mari Evans, Carolyn Rodgers, Gwendolyn Brooks, Mae Jackson, and Haki Madhubuti. Gwendolyn Brooks, who was also associated with Jack Conroy, provided a link between the 1930s Midwest radicals and those of the 1960s. Unlike the New York writers, who, with rare exceptions, were published by white companies, the writers in the Midwest established their own institutions. *Black World* was published by a black company; and Haki Madhubuti, of the 1960s Chicago group OBAC, organized Third Press, which has published the latest and perhaps one of the more formidable challengers to the New York Intellectual Superstars, Joyce Ann Joyce. She has already tangled with members of the Northeastern Talented Tenth, W. E. B. DuBois's term for the intellectual elite that would lead blacks to freedom. (The fraction one-tenth was derived from the black population's being 10 million at the time DuBois invented this concept.)

Joyce, who bears a striking resemblance to abolitionist Sojourner Truth, has shaken up black intellectual circles by challenging the most powerful P.C. group on campus: the gender feminists. Her main thesis is that the establishment has promoted black women and pushed back black male writers because, unlike black male writers, black women, in their fiction, place the issues of race and politics into the background. This charge is similar to the charges that the original worker writers of the Midwest made against the East-of-the-Hudson writers and echoes the debate between Chin and Kingston.

Joyce used my ongoing dialogue with feminists to make her point. Chicagoan Joyce said that she was misled by reviews of my work published in New York magazines and conversations with writers and critics from the African-American literary community. "One of the most important problems in scholarship on Reed," she said, "involves his negative characterizations of black women. While much emphasis is put on this idea, scholars (both male and female) overlook the fact that his male characters are no more positive than their female counterparts. Indeed, all of the characters in an Ishmael Reed novel are fair game for a Reed attack of human weakness." Joyce also agreed with Trudier Harris, a black scholar, who wrote in a controversial essay about Alice Walker's *The Color Purple* that white feminist scholars were responsible for creating a large market for books by a handful of black women, especially those who bashed black men. (Author Toni Morrison attributes the popularity of *The Color Purple* to its being championed by Gloria Steinem, identified by Michele Wallace as the gatekeeper for black feminist Divas.) "Intense media coverage and the voracious attention of white feminist scholars have been instrumental in catapulting the fiction of a select group of black women writers to the vanguard of American literature," Joyce said.

Following Joyce's remarks, the full text of which can be found in her book, the first question from the audience came from Trudier Harris. She asked Joyce why it was necessary to denigrate black women writers in order to appreciate Ishmael Reed's work. Joyce said that everything about the lives of black people was political and that black women and male writers should be viewed in the same context. She said that John A. Williams and Ishmael Reed haven't received notoriety because their work is more threatening and makes readers less comfortable than the work of black women. She went on to accuse black women critics of being soft on black women writers.

The next questioner asked Joyce what she would like to see black women critics do. She answered that they should be conscious of how their work is being used. She described Bebe Moore Campbell's work *Brothers and Sisters* as her idea of a balanced work. It was ironic that Trudier Harris would ask the question she asked. She was the first to challenge the *Ms.* magazine Hollywood steamroller that pushed *The Color Purple* not as a work of fiction, but as one reflecting black reality. It was Gloria Steinem who said that *The Color Purple* told the truth about black men. I had heard that after Harris's article was published in *Black American Literature Forum*, she had been intimidated by feminists who were outraged by her criticisms of the book.

Noticing that I was in the audience taking notes, the moderator asked whether I would like to comment on the discussion. I told her that I was covering the meeting for a newspaper and didn't want to become part of my own story, except to respond to papers on my work during a panel to which I had been invited.

I talked to Trudier Harris after the session. She said that she thought that the panel was provocative, especially the paper on Reed. She reiterated her criticism that it wasn't necessary to denigrate black women writers in order to praise Ishmael Reed. I should have asked her opinion of Henry Louis Gates Jr.'s article— an article that damaged the already weak standing of black male writers in the marketplace—published in the *New York Times Book Review*, which seemed to denigrate black men in order to praise black women. His comments were made in the course of his review of an anthology edited by Mary Helen Washington. I had seen a number of other articles and read papers that did the same thing.

I asked her whether the reported backlash against her criticism of *The Color Purple* had affected her career. She said that most of the criticism came from women who thought that since she was a black writer she shouldn't criticize a black woman writer.

They expected her to gush over Alice Walker. "I'm not a gusher," Harris said. She said that most of the denunciation of her article came from white women scholars. She put the figure at 80 percent. Harris said that she was fascinated by this response, which included personal identification with the wounded female characters and testimonies about incest and sexual violation. I asked her whether this represented a double standard. I pointed to feminists at the *Village Voice* who, over the years, have charged such diverse black male writers as Bill Gunn, John O. Killens, William Demby, Ed Bullins, Amiri Baraka, and even James Baldwin with misogyny, but praised such white male writers as William Burroughs, who was certainly no feminist. She said of course it represents a double standard.

The writer and professor bell hooks has also noticed the double standard used by white feminist academics when judging the books written by white and black male authors.

Unlike some of the other writers who've been given publicity and prominence, I'm never taken in by praise, and one of the reasons I left New York in 1967 was because I didn't want to become a showpiece, trotted out for display at literary functions, or a surrogate fronting for somebody else's political and cultural position. Though some of the small group of African-Americans who have traditionally been promoted by the segregated Literary Establishment may actually believe that all of the praise is sincere, as one who has traveled throughout the United States and read hundreds of manuscripts, I know that talent is common. Every semester I have noticed students in my classes at Berkeley whose writing is as good as anything being published, and so, though I am grateful for the many thousands of copies of my novels that have been adopted for use in college courses, I take my "canonization" with a grain of salt.

The session "Ishmael Reed: Crossing Generic Borders," in which I would face my critics without having had the opportunity to read their papers, was packed. William J. Harris of Penn State University, University Park, led with a paper called "The Flawed Heroes in the Novels of Ishmael Reed." His paper elaborated upon their flaws. The term anti-hero has been appropriated to describe such characters.

When it came to my time to respond to the papers, I agreed with Harris's observation and discussed how my characters were derived from African-American folklore, a totemic tradition that reaches back to Africa. This is perhaps true of the characters and themes in the fictional works of other African-American writers. I remember having a conversation with Toni Morrison in which she mentioned that she had found no African antecedent for the Tar Baby legend used in her book *Tar Baby*. I had read where this tale might have been influenced by the Native American Hare stories, since the Cherokee and Africans worked on the same plantations in Tennessee. Shortly before attending the MLA convention, I had discovered that the tale is from Ghana, and what threw the folklore detectives off track was that in the original story the character who becomes trapped by the sticky, gummy effigy that his enemies have created is a spider, not a hare. The tale appears in *African Folktales*, edited by Paul Radin. I maintained, in my response to Harris, that the characters in my novels belonged to the trickster tradition that one finds in both Native American and African-American folklore.

The Harris paper was followed with a paper by Virginia Whatley Smith of the University of Alabama at Birmingham. Her paper explored my novel *Mumbo Jumbo* as a hieroglyphic text, a revisionist, historical journey to the origin of Afro-Egyptian culture. It was an excellent paper, thoroughly researched and thoughtful.

In my response, I pointed out that in the 1960s, the black writers whom I knew were searching for an African civilization that would serve them as Western civilization inspired white writers. Some of us chose Egypt because its ruins seemed to rival those of

Western civilization. After traveling abroad, I found that the world was much more complicated than the one that resides in the imagination of most American intellectuals and that the term Western civilization did not reflect the diversity of European cultures, some of which did not even originate in Europe. Everywhere I traveled in Europe, I found records of the presence of Africans. Visiting Rembrandt's house last year, I read that in his time there were a number of Moors who could be seen in the streets of Amsterdam. The Moors got as far as the North Sea, and though American educators present the Moors as white, Rembrandt painted them as dark-skinned. So do the Spanish, whose culture was profoundly influenced by the African occupation of Spain. When I visited Cologne, Germany, I found pictures of Africans on the walls of its famous cathedral, and, in the museum, Roman coins with the images of Africans on them. In a Helsinki museum, I saw evidence of trade between the Vikings and North Africans.

I had always been fascinated by African sculpture and had even based my characterizations upon these models. West African sculpture, for me, was more sophisticated than the art of the Egyptians. Our missionary education never prepared us for the prospect of African civilizations other than Egypt, including Nubia, where the origin of Egyptian civilization may lie. All one has to do is consult the Internet, which doesn't wait until a crisis occurs, but covers the daily lives of Africans, to find that the media thrives on sensationalism when reporting about Africa, Public Radio International as well as National Broadcasting Company. So does the American Academy. There are still Northeastern performance intellectuals—Nathan Glazer is one—who believe that no African literature exists.

As one who struggled with the Yoruba language for ten years, under two fellowships, I assured them that this is not the case. In fact, most of those African writers who write in their native languages are unknown to the West, and Western audiences are discouraged from learning about this literature, partially due to the ignorant propaganda promoted by public intellectuals, our official

Dunciad. I am currently translating *Igbo Olodumare (God's Forest)* by D. O. Fagunwa, which is based upon 2,000 years of the oral tradition. I would rank this work next to any of the world's great epics.

Virginia Whatley Smith's explication of *Mumbo Jumbo* was refreshing, and for me it recalled a time when I was a young writer searching for a tradition I could feel good about. I've moved on since then.

With the rise of creative writing courses, the university has become a sort of patron for writers, hiring them in the same way that the Renaissance church used to hire painters and sculptors. This would seem to make for a cozy relationship, but there exists on campus popular literary theories that seem inhospitable to the writer. Some treat the writer as an anonymous donor who has no claim over the thing that he has created, about which the critic knows more than they. Critics at a conference I attended in Finland complained that the fiction writers were receiving more publicity than they. Others, whose proponents are referred to by Harold Bloom as the "School of Resentment," are more like prosecutors than critics, inspecting each book for clues to prove that the author is an enemy of their cause.

The final critic at the panel on my work was Jeff Melnick of Trinity College, who was out to convict me of misogyny. The book under examination was my novel *Reckless Eyeballing*, which was meant to be a comic sendup about the conflict, highly exaggerated in the Eastern press, between the blacks and the Jews and between black and white feminists. The portions about tensions between black and white feminists were based upon my reading of feminist publications, conversations with black feminists, and reading fiction written by feminists.

Another source was Susan Brownmiller who, in her book *Against Our Will*, excoriated Emmett Till, a youth who was murdered in the 1950s for whistling at a white woman. Brownmiller seemed to identify with his killers. She said that the Black Man encouraged rape, which, with her use of caps, was a blanket indictment of all black men. She then went on to say, in a line that most critics ignore, that when walking down the street a few years later, she was whistled at by some black men and felt "a murderous rage," which I took to suggest empathy with the killers of Till, who were seized by such a rage when Till allegedly whistled at a woman whom they considered their property. Melnick accused me of using the Brownmiller statement to indict all feminists and added that by 1986 numerous feminists had roundly criticized Brownmiller's use of the Till case. Melnick failed to mention that I was aware of the criticism of Brownmiller by Angela Davis and others and had written about it. Melnick provided no evidence that I used the statement to criticize all feminists and ignored my writings that dwelled upon the distinctions between what I call gender-first feminists, class-first feminists, and race-first feminists.

As for Susan Brownmiller, when I read her public admission that she had at one time been a prostitute, I figured that Till and "the Black Man" were paying for whatever abuses were committed against her by her pimp. Her confession reflects the kind of personal testimonies that Trudier Harris had received from white feminists about a man, or a number of men, causing them to effigize the character "Mr." in *The Color Purple*, and, I might add, Mike Tyson, Clarence Thomas, and O. J. Simpson. In my book *Reckless Eyeballing*, the narrator argues that black women writers aren't responsible for white readers generalizing about all black men on the basis of their portraits of individuals. Their own tendency to generalize about black men in interviews and articles is another matter, however. Black men taking the heat for the mistreatment of women by all men led to some curious results. Women from ethnic groups where the mistreatment of women might be worse than that of black women by black men ignored these offenses so as not to offer the group's enemies ammunition. They vented their anger against black men as a substitute for the resentments they held against their ethnic males. Black men became punching bags for the feminist movement. They were held responsible for all offenses against women. Some feminist academics and public intellectuals railed against the sexism of black male writers and black men, while fawning before famous white male writers who were notorious for their sexism. As a result of feminists exercising their rage against black men, they neglected the issues of gender relationships in their own groups, causing millions of women to suffer in silence.

When I asked Jane Mayer, who, with Jill Abrahamson, co-authored a book supporting Anita Hill's charges against Clarence Thomas, why some of the feminists, including Abrahamson, supported President Clinton during his troubles resulting from his affair with Monica Lewinsky, she said that it was hypocritical. Maybe, but another reason for the different treatment is that it's easier to float stereotypes against black men than it is against white men.

Moreover, males from other ethnic groups who might be misogynists themselves, or affiliated with institutions whose devotion to women's rights is dubious, joined in on the attack against black men. They became, all of a sudden, born-again feminists. On July 19, 2002, for example, Scott Simon and Ron Rappaport, during a broadcast on National Public Radio, criticized Tiger Woods for refusing to take a stand on whether women should be admitted to the British Open as golfers. Yet, for years, women and blacks have been suing National Public Radio, charging the outfit with racism and sexism. If Jack the Ripper were around today, he'd probably be criticizing black men for their sexism. At the conclusion of the session, I left the room with Sam Hamod, an Arab-American professor, formerly at Howard University. He was telling me how hard the job market was. He had sent out fifty applications and hadn't received any offers. Later, Hamod, a widely published poet and critic, sent me a letter from UC–Santa Cruz, which rejected his application. Santa Cruz's English department said that it was seeking younger writers to fill a creative writing job.

That night I participated in a reading at the Porter Randall Gallery in La Jolla. Among those appearing were Adrian Arancibia, Kathy Bowman, Jerome Rothenberg, and Quincy Troupe. I told

Troupe about the Asian-American panel during which Frank Chin and his ideas were denounced. Troupe told me that he had used Frank's book *Gunga Din Highway* in his class and that a number of the young Asian-American students enjoyed the book. None of Frank's novels was mentioned during the panel. Once you gain the disdain of academic feminists, you're no longer an author but a target.

The next morning, I caught the 7:45 American Airline's flight to New York. I had settled back and was writing some notes when a scholarly looking young woman, who was sitting next to me, asked me if I had attended the MLA. I had attended the MLA, covered some panels, and interviewed some people, but it wasn't until I talked to this Yale graduate student, Margaret Sabin, that I understood how dire the job situation was.

As one who receives job offers each year and who makes a substantial part of his income from writing and lectures, I have been insulated from the trials of job seeking. She made a statement to me that left me astonished. She said that of the forty Yale graduates who sought jobs this year, only four were placed. Obviously in a state of despair, she said that graduate school should be abolished, because the job market was so bad that few positions were available for many students enrolling in graduate school. Adding to this problem, foundation money was drying up. She said that the graduate students have had to commit themselves to unlimited teaching in order to support themselves. Sabin is thirty-five years old and has spent nine years in graduate school. She feels she can't ask her family to support her in graduate school any longer. When, in 1991, graduate students sought to establish a union at Yale, she said, the administration retaliated by cutting off their medical insurance, preventing them from registering in graduate school, and requiring them to pay in order to use the library. She said that graduate students were bitter. This bitterness is not only confined to graduate students at Yale.

A few semesters ago, the graduate students at Berkeley went on strike on the Berkeley campus over the issue of low wages. The administration maintained that they were not employees, but students. Sabin said that as difficult as it was for graduate students, the situation was even worse for middle-aged professors, who were out of the job market altogether. So bleak was the academic job picture that she was thinking of another profession.

The January 27 issue of the *Chronicle of Higher Education* bemoaned the growing influence of public intellectuals. The writer Theodore J. Lowi surmised that "some of the recent attention to public intellectuals can simply be attributed to journalists, who are themselves public intellectuals of a sort, welcoming bad news about academe."

Our public intellectuals often sound like crass talk-show hosts, those at the scavenger end of ideas, when characterizing the intellectual and political climate on American campuses. For example, I've noticed that after every MLA convention a public intellectual gets a sensational article published, mocking some of the titles of the panels or casting the MLA as a den of revolutionaries with tenure. (One of those who has ridiculed the MLA's attempt at inclusion is James Atlas, a writer for the *New York Times*. On February 12, 1995, Mr. Atlas wrote a puff piece about those whom he described as the Opinion Elite: "young, brainy, adversarial, who are winning the war against liberalism." Though Atlas attempted to portray himself as an outsider, the February 20, 1995, *New York Observer* revealed that he had received a grant from the conservative think tank, the Manhattan Institute, to fund a biography of Saul Bellow. Bellow's son, Adam Bellow, publisher of *The Bell Curve*, was placed at the center of this elite, in the cover picture accompanying the article.)

The real story is that the MLA is a traditional organization devoted to the maintenance of the Western Canon. Lovers of Chaucer and Shakespeare have nothing to worry about. This is the situation in high schools and colleges nationwide. According to a December 1994 survey of 527 English departments at two- and four-year institutions, conducted in the 1990–1991 school years, the writer most often included in American literature survey courses was the great

Afrocentric Nathaniel Hawthorne. His work was taught in 66 percent of courses. The list, in order of frequency, continued with Her-
man Melville, Walt Whitman, Emily Dickinson, Mark Twain, and
Ralph Waldo Emerson. The names of twenty authors, seventeen of
them male, appeared on the list before that of a black writer, Frederick Douglass. A College Board report released last year reached
similar conclusions. Ralph Ellison, a black writer, appeared thirty-
third, after a list of white writers, most of them male, that included
Twain, Hawthorne, Ernest Hemingway, Charles Dickens, Shakespeare, John Steinbeck, and F. Scott Fitzgerald.

Even with this report, I doubt whether the myth of the vanishing great white male author will subside, and some of the panic will
probably continue to be published in the *New York Times*, where
news of the survey and report appeared. As a member of the MLA,
I have examined lots of MLA material and I agree. So rather than
being a P.C. circus, the MLA is a jobs fair in a time when the jobs
just aren't there.

Though there may be some feminists who have more power on
campuses than African-Americans, Latinos, and Asian-Americans
and who insist upon political correctness, before there was ever
such a thing as feminist studies, legions of students for generations
had complained about receiving poor grades for challenging a professor's fixed views about a particular subject. Moreover, some have
even accused feminist studies of being a front for phallocentric theory. The poet and professor June Jordan said that one of the reasons
she left the women's studies department at UC–Berkeley was because she was weary of working in a department dominated by
white women who did little more than mimic the theories of
French white males. She said that the acknowledgment of black
women's culture took the form of patronizing gestures such as lav-
ishing attention upon black women celebrities invited in for tem-
porary engagements.

Though the Asian-American panel was devoted to a politically
correct line, none of the panel's members have the power to effect

university policy one way or the other. The administering of university policies is still the prerogative of middle-class white males. At the university where I teach, the faculty is 95 percent white male, yet in a messy rant printed in the *San Francisco Examiner*'s magazine section with the provocative title "Multiculturalism's Phony War with the Liberal Tradition," Gary Kamiya portrayed a Berkeley campus being threatened by a black takeover.

His argument that multiculturalism has failed because the conditions of the inner cities haven't changed was as bizarre as some of his extravagant claims about the power of the multiculturalists. The largest underclass in the United States is the white underclass, but Kamiya would never rate the success of the Eurocentric curriculum by its ability to lift the white underclass. After the standard superficial analysis of Afrocentrics and others and some pasted-in quotes from Henry Louis Gates Jr., Kamiya, in the manner of other journalists who've distorted issues like affirmative action and welfare, cited some scary tales about P.C. One of those cited was the incident during which black women challenged the ability of white women to analyze Toni Morrison's novels. In the typical hit-and-run rhetoric that characterizes the media's coverage of P.C., he said, "PC simply recapitulates (in a more pedantic and careerist, less orgiastic way) the inanities of the cultural New Left, with countercultural being replaced by 'multicultural.' But the counter was not counter, and the multi is not multi."

At one point Kamiya mentioned the American Cultures campus-wide course requirement, which was instituted at the University of California at Berkeley to satisfy student demands that there be more ethnic courses. What he failed to mention was that most of the recipients of the teaching fellowships are white and that white ethnic cultures are included in the mix of subjects that are being taught.

Among those receiving American Cultures fellowships were those who had vigorously opposed the program when it was being debated, including a professor who had written a Sunday supplement article about the dangers of multiculturalism, an article that was revealed to have been plagiarized.

During an interview that I conducted for this article, Kamiya admitted that he failed to interview a single African-American, Latino, Asian-American, or Hispanic professor, nor did he attend a single class where P.C. was running amok. He told me that he had culled most of his information about P.C. in a hurried cut-and-paste job from reading books.

One of those books that Kamiya quotes is Richard Bernstein's *The Dictatorship of Virtue*. Bernstein, book reviewer for the *New York Times*, is another journalist who substitutes rhetoric and scary anecdotes for a critical analysis of P.C. He alarms the public with frightening and ominous admonitions, using the language that the old Cold War warriors once used against the Communist menace. One wonders why Bernstein's book didn't include one of those old maps used to accompany Communist-threat film propaganda, that of multiculturalism as an octopus extending its *dark* tentacles over a map of the United States. A terrifying military-styled warning ends his book. "The multiculturalist fortress is empty. We should not flee. The battle is ours." The truculent nature of Bernstein's language confirms my suspicion that members of the media are sometimes subtly and sometimes not so subtly encouraging disgruntled whites to get physical with those whom they consider a threat to the security of some middle-class white males, not the poor ones, who, like most whites in their condition, are virtually ignored by the media.

Like Gary Kamiya, who once drew an angry letter from Al Young for concocting a quote critical of Spike Lee and attributing it to Young, Bernstein seems to have black people on his mind. In a recent *New York Times* story published on January 25, 1995, about the California initiative against affirmative action, he used one of the techniques that's been employed by conservatives and neoconservatives to embarrass blacks, comparing them unfavorably with a model minority. He wrote of Chinese parents who were suing a local San Francisco high school for placing a ceiling on the number of Chinese students being admitted so as to insure a racial balance that would include Latinos and African-Americans. Bernstein omitted any reference to Chinese-Americans benefiting from affirmative action, because in the minds of black-obsessed journalists like Bernstein, blacks are exclusively those who receive benefits from social programs, even though statistics show that the white poor have received more from government programs and the typical beneficiary of affirmative action is a white professional woman.

In San Francisco there is an organization called Chinese for Affirmative Action, and shortly after the Bernstein article appeared, Asian-American students representing Asian/Pacific Islander communities from five campuses gathered at the University of California to support affirmative action. Northeastern pundits who are full of resentment against African-Americans and constantly use the model-minority stereotype to hammer blacks might be surprised at a comment by Felicia Sze, co-chair of the Asian Pacific Council at UC–Berkeley. "A lot of us are from refugee, lower-income background and are having a hard time getting into the university."

Richard Bernstein was also an enthusiastic backer of Matty Rich's *Straight Out of Brooklyn*, a film that portrayed blacks as degenerates whose problems were traceable to bad habits being passed down through the generations. (Yet, when Andrea Dworkin challenged misogyny practiced in Israeli society, in her book *Scapegoat*, Bernstein went apoplectic in a *New York Times* review of the book.)

The favor and excessive attention that the media heap upon public intellectuals who carry on the attack against diversity can be seen in the support they gave American Enterprise Institute Fellow Lynne Cheney's criticism of the new national standards for teaching history. Her charge that the standards didn't pay enough attention to white males turned out to be false. (Here again, as with other conservatives who suffer from what I would call the Black People Fever, people who see black or a black behind society's social and cultural

woes, Cheney's complaint was about a black person, Harriet Tubman, the Underground Railroad general, receiving more attention in
the guidelines than General George Washington.)

Under questioning from Representative David Skaggs, Democrat of Colorado, during her appearance before the House Interior
Appropriations Committee, Cheney admitted that she had "read
the standards too quickly." She was roundly criticized for this de-
ception by Frank Rich of the *New York Times* and Todd Gitlin in
the *New York Observer*. Gitlin's article was entitled "History Standards: Culture Warriors Shoot First, Do Homework Later." Cheney's protest about the historical guidelines was printed in the *Wall
Street Journal*, which has a history of running unsubstantiated attacks on multiculturalism. She was provided generous time on the
television networks, including the *MacNeil/Lehrer NewsHour*,
which has broadcast numerous shows attacking multiculturalism,
and her views were supported by John Leo of *U.S. News & World
Report* and *Newsweek* and Albert Shanker, the head of the American Federation of Teachers.

After attending the MLA conference, I am more than ever
convinced that the P.C. scare is a hoax promoted by some of the
same people who raised the specter of an invincible Soviet Union.
They were wrong about the Soviet Union and they are wrong about
multiculturalism. As a result they have corrupted the discussion
about this as well as other issues: crime, welfare, illegitimacy,
among them. They are financed by powerful corporations who have
established think tanks and institutes so that they may have unlimited access to a media that endorse their opinions no matter how
far-fetched and fanciful. The damage that has been caused by their
distortions about multiculturalism can be gauged by the ignorant
letters to the editors and talk-show calls about the subject.

The public intellectuals who now attack the American campus
are of the same mentality as those who believe that the former
president and Senator Hillary Rodham Clinton murdered Vince
Foster or that crime and welfare are exclusively black issues. They

are yahoos with degrees who are battering the American university, already beset by economic problems. The situation at the University of California is so bad that some were suggesting that a state of emergency be declared. This is the situation on other campuses as well. As budget cuts are being leveled at City University of New York, professors are frantically sending out their resumes. While academic cold warriors are complaining about phantom takeovers, the American university is in peril.

Unfortunately, those who are the target of their smears have not successfully mounted a counterattack. This is because, as one scholar told me, the other side has all of the microphones. He was a native Ibo from Nigeria who had studied in Nigeria and England. He couldn't understand why there was a public impression, created by anti-multicultural organs like *Newsweek*, that affirmative action was sending droves of unqualified black professors into academe. He said that he had sent out a number of applications. All of them had been rejected.

—**An earlier version of this article
appeared in the *San Diego Reader*,
April 20, 1995**

CHAPTER 3

Can Poetry's Big Daddy Deliver San Diego?

IT'S A MOVIE YOU WILL NEVER SEE. A SMART BLACK YOUNGSTER excels at baseball and basketball, but in his twenties he becomes a poet. Quincy Troupe's career has been full of such surprises. Though he is of a build—220 pounds, six foot two—that makes him scary to many whites, he is able to persuade members of the white establishment to back his programs. Though he never viewed himself as a teacher and was, like me, drafted into the profession, he is one of the best teachers ever to set foot in an American classroom. While attending one of his classes during the writing of this article, I witnessed an amazing performance during which Troupe managed to convert his grief at the passing of three famous role models into a lesson plan about writing the personal narrative. Later, I asked a white student whether he enjoyed the class. He said, "Thoroughly," and I could tell by his expression that he meant it.

Although Troupe has dreadlocks and two missing front teeth, his bohemian appearance hasn't denied him access to the living rooms of the mighty. When he gave a party on the occasion of the publication of one of his magazines, Jacqueline Kennedy Onassis showed up. Only someone with Troupe's energy and dedication could draw thousands of people to a series of New York poetry readings sponsored by the Frederick Douglass Creative Arts Center (named for the nineteenth-century abolitionist).

Troupe wants to do the same thing in San Diego. His greatest ambition is to launch a festival, a sort of Olympics of the arts, that would join Mexico with San Diego. One could say that Troupe has been rehearsing for this project all his life.

Born in 1943 in St. Louis, Quincy Troupe was introduced to sports, multiculturalism, and literature at a very early age. His father, Quincy Sr., was the second-greatest catcher in the Negro Leagues (Josh Gibson was the first) and played with legends Satchel Paige and Cool Papa Bell. At thirty-nine Troupe Sr. made the major leagues as a catcher for the Cleveland Indians. In Monterey, in the Mexican Leagues, Roy Campanella was his backup.

As a child, Quincy accompanied his father, who spoke Spanish and French fluently, as he traveled to Mexico, Venezuela, and Cuba. As a scout for the St. Louis Cardinals, Quincy's father recommended Orlando Cepeda, Willie McCovey, Roberto Clemente, and Juan Marichal, all of whom were rejected by the Cardinals. I wonder whether his father's organizing abilities may have influenced the young Troupe. My speculation was influenced by a conversation I had with the sociologist Harry Edwards, who was praising *Miles, The Autobiography*, which Troupe brilliantly coaxed out of Miles Davis. Edwards said that the way Miles organized various musical groups was similar to the organizing techniques used in team sports. Troupe Jr., a basketball team captain who made all-state and all-Army, used his experience to organize some of the most successful New York cultural events of the '70s and '80s.

By the time Quincy Troupe was fourteen, he had read Ellison, Himes, Faulkner, and Hemingway. His mother was an avid reader, a habit that rubbed off on the youngster. He regularly received the BookWorm Prize awarded to the St. Louis student who read the most books. But it was Troupe the athlete who won a baseball and basketball scholarship to Grambling College in Louisiana.

After college, Troupe entered the Army. As part of the Army

basketball team, he traveled throughout Europe. While stationed between Metz and Paris, from 1962 to 1964, Troupe befriended Carol Anne Marie Rosiere. At the time, he was working on a novel about a young black American living in exile in Paris. Looking back upon the novel, Troupe now says that it was terrible.

Rosiere's family knew Jean-Paul Sartre, the French novelist, playwright, and existentialist philosopher, and introduced the young black American to him. Sartre took an instant liking to Troupe and invited him to his apartment, which Troupe remembers as being crammed with books and paintings, some of them by Picasso. Troupe recalls Sartre probing him about the problems faced by black Americans. The "owlish"-looking man encouraged Troupe to keep a diary.

Rosiere also introduced the budding writer to poetry, the works of Rimbaud and Baudelaire. He discovered Pablo Neruda and T. S. Eliot on his own.

About this time, Troupe suffered a knee injury that ended his basketball career, during which he regularly scored twenty-five to thirty points per game. (Troupe's not becoming a professional athlete was later a bone of contention between him and his father, who believed that he could have become a star pitcher. Interestingly, some believe that Miles Davis, his subject, who trained as a boxer, could have succeeded in that sport.)

France changed Troupe as it had changed previous generations of black Americans. On his return to the United States, he abandoned his wrinkleless style and his Quo Vadis haircut and assumed the demeanor of an outsider. He stopped wearing ties. St. Louis, in comparison to Paris, was boring and provincial. In 1964 Troupe moved to Los Angeles, where he continued writing poetry. He says it was the kind of poetry you read in the *New Yorker*, safe and well crafted.

In Los Angeles, Troupe met Bunchy Carter, the famous Southern California representative of the Black Panther Party who was later killed during a shoot-out with members of Maulana Karenga's

Us, an organization associated with cultural nationalism. At a poetry reading, Troupe heard Ojenke, a powerful performance poet, and decided that he wanted to write like him. Troupe became part of a circle of writers who would come to be known as the Watts Poets and Writers: K. Curtis Lyle, Elaine Brown (who would later become chairperson of the Black Panther Party when Huey Newton was an exile in Cuba), poet Jayne Cortez, novelist Louise Merriweather, and Stanley Crouch were also members of the group.

Troupe remembers Crouch, who would in 1980 endorse Ronald Reagan in glaring *Village Voice* headlines, as having a different attitude in those days. But, says Troupe, "I gathered even then that he would do anything it took to get over, even if it meant selling somebody down the river." A later incident would so rupture the relationship between Troupe and Crouch that Troupe would vow never to speak to Crouch again.

In 1966 Troupe and some of his colleagues—painters, musicians, and writers—began a commune that operated out of 9807 Beach Street, in Watts. They took turns working and paying bills for the operation, which they named the House of Respect. The commune lasted for a year and a half, until it was destroyed by an arsonist. While living in the commune, Troupe wrote every day. "I got to be pretty good," Troupe says of this period. After leaving the House of Respect, Troupe moved into East L.A.

In the aftermath of the 1965 Watts riots, which Troupe witnessed, screenwriter and novelist Budd Shulberg helped to found the famous Watts Writers Workshop. It was through Budd Shulberg that Troupe obtained his first reading tour.

During 1968 he read his poetry at Kansas State, Howard University, and Dartmouth College. Troupe supported his household by writing articles for the *Los Angeles Free Press* and the *Los Angeles Sentinel*. He wrote about community issues and about black musicians like Ornette Coleman, assignments that were to prepare him to compose one of the most successful oral autobiographies ever to appear in book form. His personal acquaintance with black music and musicians would also contribute to the forming of *Miles, The Autobiography*.

These friendships were formed in St. Louis after Troupe's mother married a musician who performed at a club called The Riviera. When famous musicians came through town, they would visit the Troupes. He saw Sam Cooke, Muddy Waters, Lightnin' Hopkins, Jackie Wilson, Ike and Tina Turner, Charlie Parker, and Miles Davis at clubs like the Glass Bar. The King of Rock and Roll, St. Louis resident Chuck Berry, was considered a local.

In 1968 a white teacher, whose name Troupe has forgotten, asked him whether he would like to teach. Quincy Troupe's teaching career began at UCLA's Upward Bound program. The curriculum included works by Richard Wright, Ralph Ellison, Gwendolyn Brooks, and Amiri Baraka. In retrospect, Troupe believes that initially he was confrontational with the white students but later learned a more balanced approach so that "I wouldn't just insult the white kids while letting the black students get away with things." His next teaching assignment took him to Ohio University in Athens, Ohio.

After Athens, around 1971, Troupe moved to New York and taught at Richmond College (later to become the College of Staten Island). He then moved to the Upper West Side of Manhattan, living on Central Park West and then at 846 West End Avenue. Toni Morrison worked on her book *Tar Baby* while subletting that apartment from Troupe. His parties were usually packed with a who's who of the black New York art world.

In 1973 Troupe met Fred Hudson, director of the Frederick Douglass Creative Arts Center, who invited him to teach poetry at the center. It was in this role that Troupe began to organize readings that, over the years, would draw thousands of black New Yorkers to hear the major writers of African-American literature and Quincy's workshop students. Only Ralph Ellison and Alice Walker declined to participate. Troupe calls Pulitzer Prize winner and MacArthur Fellow James Allan McPherson an "asshole" for first committing himself to a reading and then not showing. National Book Award winner Charles Johnson also backed out at the last minute.

The first of what would become known as the Black Roots Festival was an all-day event held at the Cathedral of St. John the Divine, near Columbia University, in 1973. Later the readings were held at Columbia and at the Society for Ethical Culture. The publication of three books of poetry gave a significant boost to Troupe's career. The first was *Embryo*, published in 1972.

I first heard Troupe read in 1969 during an African-American conference in Buffalo, New York. At the time, I dismissed him as a "riot" poet, one who was a good performer but whose writing wouldn't work on the page. I walked out after about three poems. Later, after reading his poems, I decided that I had been wrong. Troupe has that rare gift, the ability to transfer his sound to the page. He had more in common with Cuban poet Nikolas Guillen than with the Last Poets, '60s precursors of rap.

Though he is capable of writing tender love poems and meditative poems about such subjects as his family, the typical Troupe poem comes at the reader like a locomotive on fire, full of blazing and powerful imagery, like that favored by the Expressionist painters who broke with the tradition that a work of art should be concerned with beauty. Troupe's poetry abounds in images of "darkness, razors, blood, bone, roaches, quivering pus, maggot-swarming words, monstrous bugs." He is one of America's handful of authentic jazz poets, a category that's much abused by critics, especially those who wish to expropriate black forms.

Steve Cannon, a New York professor and playwright, and I published Troupe's second and third books of poetry, *Snake-Back Solos* (1979) and *Skulls Along the River* (1984). I could tell by the response to the books—hundreds of people attended the New York book parties—that Troupe was a poet with the potential to draw a popular and mixed audience.

For Troupe, 1989 was a bittersweet year, a year that saw him catapulted into international fame and the year in which his son was arrested on a rape charge. The hippest salon in New York had moved uptown to Harlem, where Quincy and his wife, Margaret, took a ten-room apartment with four fireplaces in a building that once served as the Astors' summer place and more recently as the setting for the film *New Jack City*. Troupe was teaching at Columbia's graduate writing program as well as at Staten Island.

The year began with a controversy. Troupe appeared on the cover of *Poets and Writers* magazine, which also carried an interview. Troupe drew the ire of a number of academics with his comment that most American poetry was boring because it was written by people whose lives were boring.

The Legacy, a book of essays about James Baldwin, edited by Troupe, also appeared in 1989. He had scored a coup by obtaining Baldwin's deathbed interview. He had asked Baldwin to identify the person who, in recent years, had hurt him the most, and Baldwin mentioned my name. I had hurt him, he said, because I had called him a "cocksucker." I was shocked. I hadn't seen Baldwin since about 1979, when he visited the University of California at Berkeley, a visit that I helped to arrange. The poet Sarah Fabio, then terminally ill with cancer, and I had also arranged for him to attend a community meeting at a black church. Baldwin and his companions arrived three hours late, even though they were within the vicinity of the church. By then, the church was almost empty because I had told the congregation to go home. When Baldwin and his party finally arrived at the church, I was livid and some words were exchanged, but I didn't call him a cocksucker. When he broke into tears, I calmed down and took him out for a drink.

This was the second time Baldwin had made an engagement that I had arranged, only to break his word. In 1964 I organized a party for him and he didn't show. I was devastated.

Baldwin's last interview with Troupe put me in a lose-lose situation. If I had challenged Baldwin's account, it would appear as though I were disputing the word of a dead man. The incident marked me as a homophobe, and since then I've been a target for the gay contingent of African-American letters, both closeted and out.

The beginning of the end of Troupe's relationship with Stanley Crouch also came about this time. Troupe was one of those who had been designated as a pallbearer by James Baldwin. Maya Angelou, Sonia Sanchez, Max Roach, and Toni Morrison were also enlisted. According to Troupe, he and others watched with disgust as Crouch opportunistically muscled himself into the line reserved for the pallbearers. The deed was made more "terrible" in Troupe's eyes by an article published in the *Village Voice* after the funeral, in which Crouch trashed James Baldwin.

The final split occurred when Crouch accused Troupe of plagiarizing from Jack Chambers's 1983 book *Milestones* in *Miles*. At first, Troupe says, Crouch praised the book, but when Troupe heard that Crouch had been assigned to review the book for the *Village Voice*, Troupe says he knew Crouch would produce a negative review. As for the charge of plagiarism, Troupe says that Jack Chambers called him and praised the book. According to Troupe, this wasn't the first time that Crouch had praised something in private, yet trashed it when hired to write about it. Troupe recalls Crouch's glowing account of his trip to Africa, only to read Crouch's negative account of his experience in the *Village Voice*.

After that, Troupe vowed never to speak to Crouch again, and in a sort of farewell-to-New York article that appeared in *Newsday* shortly before Quincy and Margaret moved to San Diego, Troupe warned that Crouch was a pit bull who is kept chained in a dungeon by some members of the neoconservative Jewish right, only to be let out once in a while to attack famous blacks or those literary blacks whom the neoconservatives feel are their main competition in the world of New York literary politics, as well as in the literary marketplace.

Outspoken and maverick, Quincy Troupe is one of the few black intellectuals to challenge the power of the New Black Elite, who, whether right wing or "progressive," have forged a consensus around the notion that whatever problems blacks face do not arise from racism, unemployment, the breakdown of the agricultural community that provided the mainstay for African-Americans from the time of the free-market West African societies, the replacement of manual labor by machines, the moving of jobs from the cities to the suburbs, and so on, but from the personal behavior of blacks or from something going on inside them, "self-loathing" or a "culture of poverty." Like the white critics of black personal behavior, the members of the elite have access to generous cash allotments in the form of grants and other perks and are provided space in publications to break the careers of other blacks; but unlike the conservative whites, who are permitted to comment about a range of subjects, the sponsors of black conservatives require that they criticize other blacks and remain silent about the social pathologies that may exist among other groups.

They can denounce rap music but have to hold their fire when it comes to criticizing the misogynist attitudes that exist in heavy metal or country-western music. They can recommend that Norplant, a birth-control drug with dangerous side effects, be given to "promiscuous" black women but dare not suggest on the *New York Times* op-ed page that white women, who account for the fastest rising rate of out-of-wedlock births, be given the same equipment.

Troupe calls them Reconstructed Negroes. One of those Reconstructed Negroes, a black whom the establishment finds acceptable because his views are closely aligned with its views, is Gerald Early, Stanley Crouch's protege, whom Troupe refers to as "William Gass and Daniel Halpern's Negro." Though members of the New Black Elite like Early may assume a public posture of cosmopolitanism, lashing out at Afrocentrism and multiculturalism on the op-ed pages, when it comes to their own personal ambitions, their supporters are not above playing the race card. Early's assignment seems to be that of maintaining the status quo literary values from a posture that transcends race; however, Halpern and Denise Levertov petitioned Quincy Troupe, who was judge for a literary contest in which Early was a nominee, to award the prize to Early on the grounds that he was black. Troupe refused to do so and awarded the prize to a white poet, whom he felt had produced work superior to Early's.

Troupe experienced the highs and lows of being a star on the New York literary scene. The crack epidemic had reached Graham Court, where he lived, and threatened the security of his family. He found himself spending more time in a Petionville condominium located in the mountains above Port-au-Prince, Haiti. At first, he said, he and Margaret were always relieved upon returning to New York, but as social conditions in that city began to deteriorate, the situation changed. He began to dread returning home. (The Troupes gave up the condominium when Haitian President Aristide was ousted by a coup.)

The year 1989 also saw the publication of *Miles, The Autobiography*. Miles Davis was Troupe's early hero, as well as mine. As a teenager living in Buffalo, New York, I not only listened to bebop, but talked, walked, and dressed bebop. Bebop was a way of life. When I met Max Roach, I told him that he and the beboppers kept me and my friends out of reform school because we spent our teenage years in each other's homes listening to bebop.

From the very beginning, the musician and the writer had hit it off. Troupe had been assigned by *Spin* magazine to interview Miles Davis. They spent ten hours together. Soon they had established such a rapport that they could communicate without talking. For this reason, Troupe used the first person in writing the book, because he had successfully tapped into the Miles style. "I was the vessel through which his memoirs flowed," as Troupe put it while lecturing to his class on the personal narrative. He was able to mime Miles's language and his attitudes so that there was nothing of Troupe in the book. "If you're going to write another person's autobiography, your job is to be a technician," he told the class. "You must make it comprehensible, readable, and digestible."

Many people were offended by the autobiography's scatology,

even Troupe's brother, a minister. But Troupe defended Davis's use of obscenity. "This is the way St. Louis jazz men talk. My father's generation talked this way." Troupe felt that in order to be faithful to his task, he had to show Miles unabridged. *Miles, The Autobiography* became a 4-million-copy bestseller—and one of the literary events of the year, receiving rave reviews from some critics, but condemnation from others. Some of the critics were unhappy, Troupe claims, because Miles hadn't chosen them to write his autobiography.

This heady year, during which Troupe appeared on the *Today* show, produced two books, and was the subject of a Bill Moyers television profile, also included a tragic incident from which the Troupe family has yet to recover.

For Quincy Troupe and many others of his generation and mine, Miles was the epitome of the black man who didn't take any shit from anybody. Critics often described Miles's style as that of a man walking on eggshells. Miles was secretive and disdainful of those who tried to pry into the details of his personal life. He, in a sense, lived inside a shell. It was Quincy Troupe who explored the interior of the shell, revealing information about Miles Davis that only his intimates were aware of, and then some. None of the critics of Troupe's book, including Crouch, who once referred to Miles Davis as a "swine," had ever gotten that close.

The Miles of Troupe's book is basically a shy person who developed a reputation for "cursing out everybody." Instead of the arrogant, difficult personality of the public Davis legend, Troupe found in Miles someone who would even cook for you. He was, according to Troupe, a straightforward, beautiful guy. While working on the book, Troupe and Miles became good friends. Miles Davis insisted that Troupe, a fellow St. Louisan, write the book. The choice was perfect. Davis poured out his soul to Troupe, discussing his music in very technical terms, confessing to his bouts with drugs and his cruel treatment of women.

Some African-American male intellectuals feel that the white, middle-class-led feminist movement has singled out black men for the offense of misogyny while ignoring the misogyny of men who share their backgrounds. Spike Lee was criticized as a misogynist for the portrayal of women in his movies, yet little has been said of the portrayal of white women as "natural resources" in *Rising Sun* or *Crimes and Misdemeanors*, which argues that the way to deal with an independent woman is to murder her and get off, the same premise of *Presumed Innocent*. (A *San Francisco Chronicle* writer recently joined the white nationalist effort to crown Eminem the King of Hip Hop. While the misogyny of black rappers has become part of a national debate, she made very little mention of Eminem's.)

Frank Sinatra's misogyny was legendary. According to Kitty Kelly's biography of the singer, he once pushed a woman through a plate glass window, yet Sinatra was given a moving tribute by feminists at National Public Radio when he died. Some of National Public Radio's feminists are notorious black male haters.

In 1989 this singling out of black men by the feminist movement as the main perpetrators of misogyny affected the Troupe family personally. In March of that year, a coed at State University of New York at Stony Brook announced that she had been raped. A week later, Quincy Brandon Troupe, Quincy's son, was arrested. Troupe was in Detroit at the time signing copies of his anthology, *The Legacy*, and reading from his work at Wayne State University when he heard of the charges. On the night the alleged rape was supposed to have happened, Brandon was home helping the family prepare for his brother Porter's birthday party.

There was no evidence whatsoever to prove the charge, yet black and white campus feminists lined up behind the alleged rape victim. They agreed with Anita Hill that the woman should always be believed. Though the charges were eventually dropped, the episode was an ordeal for the Troupe family. By this time, Troupe's celebrity deprived him of the anonymity that he had once enjoyed. People recognized him on the street, and he was besieged by autograph seekers. He was now also accosted by those who believed that his son was guilty, regardless of the facts. Troupe chased a man from a subway car because the man had made a remark about his son's guilt. While entering a prison, where he conducted workshops, in the company of a crew from Bill Moyers's show, a guard made a remark, and Troupe collared him. Other guards had to separate them.

With his new loss of privacy, the rise of crack addiction in his neighborhood, and the publicity that accompanied the unsubstantiated charges against his son, it was only a matter of time before the Troupes would leave New York.

When I visited the Troupes in their new home on Nautilus Street in La Jolla, I was struck by how much the setting, with its surrounding hills and view of the ocean, resembled Petionville, the home of the Haitian elite. Even the style of the home, a white jellyroll-shaped Bauhaus number, which was designed to receive the maximum light, reminded me of a Petionville villa. The home is filled with paintings by well-known white, African-American, Cuban, and Haitian artists. The Troupes say they didn't experience a single instance of racism while they searched for a home in La Jolla, which has a reputation for being a sort of white-only upper-crust enclave. It is from this base that the Troupes direct their activities as movers and shakers in the communities of La Jolla and San Diego. He is professor of literature and creative writing at UCSD and is an adviser to its Helen Edison Lecture Series. He is also the curator of the Artists on the Cutting Edge Series at the Museum of Contemporary Art, San Diego. His appointment to this post came about as a result of an invitation from director Hugh Davies, whom Troupe met at a party. He gave Troupe the autonomy to design a program that has brought in such famous literary figures as Nobel Prize winner Toni Morrison, Victor Cruz, Fanny Howe, and Jerome Rothenberg. Toni Morrison read on a program that included the legendary drummer Max Roach. Next year's lineup will include Margaret Atwood, Kathy Acker, Anne Waldman, Allen Ginsberg, Oscar Hijuelos, Joy Harjo, Jessica Hagedorn, John Ashbery, and Walter Mosely.

Unlike the selfish New Black Elite who write about the problems of the inner city from Harvard and from well-heeled bohemian digs, Troupe, who even at the height of New York literary success made a decision to live in an underclass environment in Harlem, extends his generosity to the San Diego black community. He is an adviser to the Sankofa Bird project, which brings writers and thinkers to the downtown black community. He has also begun a reading skills project aimed at black men, called Brother to Brother. African-American male literary culture is on the brink of extinction as a result of the belief held by feminists and powerful black male literary critics that the achievements of black women writers may only be gained by the denigration of black male writers. Quincy Troupe believes that the only way a black male literary culture can be sustained is by getting black men to read. He says that he already has a waiting list.

In my first interview with Troupe he spoke of his great admiration for his father, Quincy Sr. The next morning he was informed that his father, who had been placed in a convalescent home, had died. It was during this lecture, delivered in a state of grief, that I understood why Troupe is such an effective teacher. He humanizes the classroom. If more and more students are refusing to enter college or are dropping out, it's because the professors have made it clear that they're not interested in them. For many professors, research, much of it duplicative of the work of others, is of prime importance, while teaching chores have been handed over to assistants, some of whom are of the same age group as the students. My most memorable teachers were those who not only put their hearts and souls into their work but loved the subject matter and teaching. Troupe knows his stuff and can lecture on the Villanelle as well as Langston Hughes's use of the blues.

Troupe, in obvious emotional pain, lectured about writing honestly, the poet versus the tyrant, the dance styles of Latin America, and shooting sports films and provided anecdotes about the womanizing habits of Pablo Neruda, Miles Davis, and his father.

Neruda, Troupe said, taught him that you could write about anything, including the fungi between your toes. It was truly amazing to watch.

The class was reading Pablo Neruda's memoirs, and at points during the lecture, they asked technical questions about Neruda's approach to writing the personal narrative and about the writing of the Davis book.

At one point during the lecture Troupe said that he at first didn't want to attend his father's funeral, but that morning Margaret said that he had to go because the funeral was what gave life closure. He said that Margaret was very wise.

Brainy, glamorous, ambitious, inventive, Margaret Troupe met Quincy Troupe at a New York poetry reading. Poet Jose Figeroa was reading, and a friend invited her to come along. Margaret was introduced to Quincy. She remembers placing her hand on his thigh and being given a hostile look by Troupe. She was so embarrassed that she went out to hail a cab, only to have Troupe approach the cab and ask her for chewing gum.

Quincy remembers it this way. He was the only other non–Puerto Rican appearing at a poetry reading. He noticed a black woman sitting in the audience and planned to talk to her but was diverted by Stanley Crouch. By the time he got to where she was, she'd left. He blamed Stanley for his missing her, and Stanley, to compensate, invited him to the Tin Palace for dinner. It was there that he was introduced to Margaret.

Margaret Porter Troupe hails from Gloster, Mississippi. She went to New York in 1969 and graduated from Iona College in New Rochelle, a New York City suburb. After being robbed there, she decided to move to New York City, where she got a job with the *New York Times* in the ad department. Porter Troupe was born to Quincy and Margaret in 1983. Quincy and poet Calvin Hernton had gone out for a drink the night her water broke, and when he returned home at 1 a.m., he had to rush her to the hospital. After all-day labor that ended in Margaret having a C-section, Porter was born. Troupe recalls that the child came out looking as if to say, "So this is what I've been waiting nine months for?"

Though the Troupes miss New York's convenience of walking to shop, the cultural life, and their friends, they enjoy San Diego's slow pace and the politeness of its residents who, like Southerners, may not like you but are civil nevertheless, whereas, in New York, people are rude and often callous. It was in La Jolla that Margaret met Drina Krimm, a real estate agent who helped the Troupes find a house. In 1991 they opened the Porter Randall Gallery on La Jolla Boulevard.

Among the major painters who have exhibited there are Oliver Jackson, Mary Lovelace O'Neal, Emilio Cruz, Jaune Quick-to-See, and Felipe Almada. Exhibits mounted by the gallery have received rave notices. Terry McMillan, Bradford Morrow, George Lewis, Sherley Anne Williams, Lynn Luria Sukenick, and Jesus Papoleto Melendez are writers who have read from their work at the gallery.

These activities and requests for his appearances keep Troupe on the road, traveling throughout the United States and Europe. Earlier this year he visited the Netherlands and Montreaux, Switzerland. Quincy Jones has requested that he write the official history of the Montreaux Jazz Festival series.

The motion picture version of *Miles, The Autobiography*, starring Wesley Snipes, whose script Troupe has already begun with Pulitzer Prize–winner Charles Fuller, will add to his busy schedule. That schedule is destined to become even busier as Troupe begins to organize an event that could make San Diego a cultural hub of the West. (In June 2002, Quincy Troupe was selected by Gov. Gray Davis to be poet laureate of California.)

—**An earlier version of this article
appeared in the *San Diego Reader*,
December 16, 1993**

CHAPTER 4

Another Day at the Front

THREE AFRICAN-AMERICAN WRITERS, PATRICIA WILLIAMS, Lee Hubbard, and Cecil Brown, have complained about taking younger relatives to see George Lucas's *The Phantom Menace* only to have these children exposed to stereotypical images of African-Americans. I'm glad that the children saw this movie in the company of these writers, who can prepare them for the combat they must wage in a society where media, including Hollywood, television, and the newspapers, present African-Americans as Faces of the Enemy, the typical portrait of African-Americans being similar to those found in a book entitled *Faces of the Enemy* by Sam Keen. This book dealt with propagandistic portraits of the Japanese, who, at that time, were engaged in hostilities against the United States. But the faces could well be those of African-Americans, who are often shown as inferior and simian and a threat to European women. A poster showing a Japanese soldier carrying a nude white woman over his shoulder is consistent with the images thrown up by the Bush family's Willie Horton campaign, which featured a black man who raped a white woman while on prison furlough. After this ad appeared, designed to link the rapist to candidate Michael Dukakis, support for Bush among Southern white men rose 20 percent, according to Willie Brown, the mayor of San Francisco.

Each day, African-Americans are confronted with hostilities

from their fellow white citizens who see themselves as unofficial deputies. I experienced an incident while working on this essay.

On July 6, I drove to the home of author Cecil Brown, who had had an encounter with the police at a swimming pool used by the University of California faculty. I had published a poem about the incident, "Strawberry Creek," in my zine, *Konch*. When this poem appeared in the local newspaper, the University of California police charged that Cecil Brown had been a menace to the women (white) bathers at the pool, although when Brown had asked the supervisor of the pool why the pool personnel had called the police, the supervisor couldn't give a reason. The police put out this story, I believe, because they wanted to cover their embarrassment at having harassed Brown, a Berkeley faculty member who had the temerity to use this pool, where one rarely sees a black person.

When I arrived at Brown's apartment at the Emeryville Water-gate, I didn't find his name listed on the directory of the building where I usually met him for our walk around the Emeryville Marina, during which, from time to time, we are put under surveillance by the Emeryville police. I returned home to call Brown and he said he'd forgotten to tell me that he had moved to another apartment in the building and that he hadn't yet received a directory number.

We decided to meet in front of the building. During my first trip, I'd noticed a police car parked at the end of my block. When I left the block to meet Cecil, for the second time, the car followed me, changing lanes as I changed lanes and finally making a dramatic left turn after it was parallel to the left side of my car. I had been around longer than the children getting initiated into American racism by exposure to the propaganda arm of the occupation, Hollywood, and so I saw my encounter with the policeman as a skirmish. A strafing. Sort of like when an innocent passenger jet enters an unfriendly territory and is buzzed by fighter jets.

This policeman was a descendant of the white patrollers whom Booker T. Washington and others complained about. The patrollers' job was to regulate the comings and goings of African slaves in the same way the UC–Berkeley police and the policeman on my block were regulating Cecil Brown and my comings and goings. The irony is that I have been the neighborhood block captain. As part of my job, I had complained to the police and to my councilperson about a pest house at a nearby intersection. It continues to be a safe haven for drug dealers and small-time criminals.

An exterminator who rid my house of rats said that the infestation had begun at this pest house, due to the young owner's unsanitary habits and the steady flow of young men who could be seen entering and exiting the house at any time during the day and night. A young man harassed my oldest daughter, Timothy, a novelist, as she walked past the house. This situation has been going on for a year and yet the police found the time to tail me while nothing was being done to close this pest house. This is a fact of everyday life in the inner city. The people who sit on their fake genteel behinds in their Upper West Side apartments, paid for by their intellectual treachery, earning their living by writing "tough love" op-eds for the *New York Times*, haven't the slightest idea about what goes on in these neighborhoods, the subject of their fatuous musings.

Unlike the youngsters who accompanied the three intellectuals to see the Lucas movie, my first experience with organized hatred against African-Americans was not with Hollywood, but with the police. It occurred on Elm Street in Chattanooga, Tennessee. I was about three years old and the police were called out ostensibly to get rid of a pack of dogs that had been disturbing the neighborhood. We were told to remain inside. The police invaded the black neighborhood and began shooting up the place. It didn't occur to me at the time, and none of my relatives read anything into it, but now that I look back upon it, this was probably like war games. The police wanted to demonstrate their firepower to a neighborhood that might become troublesome. It was an act of intimidation. Most if not all of the riots that occurred during the sixties were the result of a police incident. These uprisings should be viewed as a stateside *intafada*.

While growing up in Buffalo, New York, I, like most black male youngsters I knew, was often stopped by the police. I never gave it much thought, but it occurs to me that these were sort of checkpoint incidents. Small-scale border incidents. In many countries where the majority is at war with the minority, minority members must constantly show their I.D.'s to the occupation forces located in their neighborhoods. When they venture from their neighborhoods and are found to be in enemy territory, which is how Cecil Brown and many other black men have found themselves, they must show proof of who they are, just as free African-Americans had to constantly show their papers before abolition. Sometimes, when I'm driving through white California towns, I find myself being followed by the police from the time I enter until the time I exit the town. It's as though the Black Codes of the late nineteenth century were still in operation.

I lived in Buffalo from the time I was four until I was twenty-two and became conscious of the role of the police when I began working for the newspaper, the *Empire Star*. At thirteen I was a "printer's devil" under a staff of black intellectuals led by A. J. Smitherman, who, when a newspaperman in Tulsa, Oklahoma, had been run out of town during the Tulsa riots and charged with inciting a riot. The Afro-American newspapers, which I used to deliver, filled in the gaps about issues connected to being black in the United States that weren't covered by my "formal education."

While attending the University of Buffalo in the late 1950s, I became acquainted with some Irish-American students who were in contact with members of Buffalo's bohemia. Black and white bohemians began to intermingle and would sometimes party together. I remember on several occasions our cars being tailed by the Buffalo police. Like the "patrollers" of old, they knew their mandate: to confine black people to Black Belts and to monitor any signs of integration. White women have told me stories about being stopped by police when out on a date with black men. That's one of the reasons that Mark Fuhrman, whom F. Lee Bailey still maintains planted evidence in the O. J. Simpson case, is so popular with the American public. Fuhrman said that if he saw a black man and a white woman riding in the same car, he would stop them for no reason. (Yet, it was revealed during the trial that he had dated a black woman.)

In 1960, out of college and married, I returned to writing for the newspaper that had been run by A. J. Smitherman. Smitherman, who, in Tulsa, Oklahoma, practiced the armed self-defense that others only talked, and who was persecuted all of his life, had died and a young man named Joe Walker was now the editor. We reported about police brutality, segregation, and politics. I wrote one story about the attack against black prostitutes by the Buffalo police. "Cops and Dogs Attack Innocent Girls on High Street," was the headline, and in small type, I added "mothers say." I had interviewed one woman's mother as she left church services. The police were offended and got a black councilman to try to get me to soften my views about the police. I didn't.

My experience with the Buffalo police was mild in comparison with an ugly event that took place in New York City, where the former dictator/mayor endorsed the actions of the elite patrol, a sort of white Tonton Macoutes that has stopped and frisked thousands of black and Hispanic men. Rudolph Giuliani gets credit by white nationalist journalists for lowering the crime rate, when this trend was begun under David Dinkins, whose administration saw the New York crime rate reduced to the lowest level since 1936. (Even the *New York Times*, which inflames its white readers with generalizations about African-Americans in almost every section of the newspaper, gave credit to Dinkins for lowering the crime rate, yet journalists E. J. Dionne and Cokie Roberts erroneously reported that crime had gone up during Dinkins's term. Dionne said "skyrocketing," which was untrue.)

I figured something was corrupt about the New York police when, after the woman I was living with was robbed a couple of times, the police who took the report came back and asked for dates. This is what a New York columnist must have meant when he discussed New York cops having girlfriends in the city and visiting their families on the weekend.

It was in New York that I discovered historical ethnic divisions that colored the relations between the police, blacks, and Puerto Ricans. The cops were members of the Irish- and Italian-American upper underclass who, as one former police commissioner said, were from authoritarian backgrounds. I also found that whites, no matter how radical, were generally treated better by the police than blacks. The late Abbie Hoffman, the founder of the Yippies and author of *Steal This Book,* said in the *New York Times Magazine* that he had a nephew/uncle relationship with the commander of the precinct located on the Lower East Side. I was beaten up there and so were other blacks, men and women.

I was between jobs, having been laid off by Tri State Transportation, a firm that was doing a traffic analysis of the New York City area. While living in New York, I worked in factories and hospitals, as a clerk at the New York State Department of Labor, and a couple of times knocked on doors gathering information for the *Daily News* straw polls. I'd spend my leisure time writing poetry, and socializing at Stanley's, a bar on Avenue B where artists, writers, and musicians would hang. Some of my friends were members of the Umbra workshop, a group of black novelists and poets who met weekly to examine each other's work. One day, (the late) Calvin Hernton, a poet and sociologist, Duncan Roundtree III, and I were walking down Avenue B. We were in a jovial mood. I had been reading a series in the *New York Times* about police corruption that had been exposed by the Knapp Commission. One memorable line in the piece went, "They're taking bribes in low places." When I saw two cops carrying something wrapped in paper bags out of the Annex bar, which was owned by the late Mickey Ruskin, I turned to Calvin and said, "The *Times* is right. They 're taking bribes in low places." I said it within the earshot of the two policemen, but didn't think they'd heard me. We kept walking. Calvin said something to a woman who was walking on the other side of the street. I don't remember her saying anything, but she wasn't offended. She smiled.

The next thing I knew the police were speeding toward where we were walking. They leaped out of the car and put the three of us in. They took us to the police station that was commanded by the man Abbie Hoffman said reminded him of an uncle. I was put into a separate room at the request of the cop, let's call him Officer Shrunk, who, on the way to the station, kept going on about how he didn't want black guys dating his wife or daughter. Even the other cop looked at him funny. This cop said he wanted to deal with the "nigger" who was wearing the blue shirt. That was me. Shortly after this, I was isolated from Calvin and Duncan. The cop came into the room and began punching me out. I burst into tears, because I was frustrated. My urge was to smash him like one would a termite or an ant, but I had enough sense to restrain myself. He had the guns. And I knew that if I struck him I could be killed or accused of resisting arrest. These are some of the tricks that the police use to add more blacks to the prison population, one of the facts ignored by people like criminologist James Q. Wilson and Sam Roberts of the *New York Times*, who believe that blacks are genetically prone to violence. (Wilson has been provided a forum by CNN to broadcast his views to 200 countries.) Officer Shrunk had the power, I had nothing but my wit, and ultimately my wit would get me out of this jam. This miserable human being was intent upon ruining us, because I had made a dumb remark, which he'd overheard. So malicious and sick was this person that he searched us hoping to find some reefer so that he could really stick it to us.

Shortly after we were taken from this station presided over by a benevolent uncle, where white cops called us "niggers" while the black cops went about their work, saying nothing, the Shrunk came into my cell at the Tombs, a city prison whose gothic style mirrors the state of our racist and primitive criminal justice system. By contrast to the fierce person with the contorted face who'd beaten me at the police station, the man before me was very polite. He said that if I pled guilty to disorderly conduct I'd only spend a weekend at Rikers Island, the medieval outfit where New York prisoners are stored. I told him that I wasn't going to plead guilty to anything. (Years later, I learned from a British documentary about the New York criminal justice system that indigent blacks were urged to plead guilty whether they were guilty or not, another reason for the high incarceration of blacks that will never be analyzed by the army of intellectual sluts who get paid by think tanks to recycle the same old lies about African-Americans, yet call the African-American "underclass" lazy.) Officer Shrunk got mad and left the cell in a huff. I learned later that the details of the incident had gotten around, and when we were released some black cops asked us to tell the story about the incident that led to our being jailed. They thought that it was funny. A Catholic priest whom I shall never forget visited my cell and asked if there was someone whom he could call on my behalf. I gave him the number of the woman I was living with. We were charged with disorderly conduct, the kind of all-purpose charge that's used to satisfy a policeman's black and Hispanic quotas, similar to the Black Codes that the KKK in the South used to contain African-Americans. Duncan Roundtree had to spend the weekend in jail and since I was obviously the target of the policeman's malice and hatred, I raised the bail for him. I borrowed the money from the daughter of one of New York's most prominent capitalists; she had devoted time and effort to the civil rights struggle only to become cynical. She told me in the mid-sixties that most white people don't care whether blacks live or die. She was right. That night, as soon as I got home, the Catholic priest called and asked if I was all right.

The courts kept postponing our trial because Officer Shrunk repeatedly failed to show up. This, I was to learn later, was a vindictive way of running up our lawyers' bills. Finally the day of the trial arrived. I put on a three-piece pin-striped suit and sat patiently until our case was called. When it was, the charges against Calvin and Duncan were dismissed. The so-called American criminal justice system was going to try me for the crime slaves used to get whipped for, sassing white folks. I took the stand. The trial took place about a month after the first demonstration against the Vietnam War had taken place in Times Square, and seated behind me were about thirty cops who were there to testify against the demonstrators whom they had arrested.

I pointed to the two cops who were sitting below the judge's bench and told him that I'd seen them taking bribes out of the Annex, and that because I had called them on it, they had arrested us and beaten me. My testimony got good to me and some of the black people and Puerto Rican people in the courtroom began to make sounds of approval, egging me on. I was venting the rage that had been building up inside me for months. The blacks and Hispanics knew what I was talking about. A number of them had also been set up, been victims of what amounted to paramilitary search-and-destroy missions. I was calm and precise and pulled up a strength that I didn't know I had. When I finished, the two officers, who, at the beginning of the trial were smirking, were now glaring at me.

When I sat down, I felt a wave of hostility aimed at my direction from the cops who were there to testify against the anti-war protesters. They'd probably lie too. When I was asked to stand to hear the judge's verdict, I was calm and prepared to take what was coming to me. The judge said "Guilty." But when my lawyer asked for the sentence, the judge almost ran from the courtroom! My lawyer, his last name was Green, stood with his mouth open. The sight of the judge fleeing the courtroom without sentencing me stunned him. He said he'd never seen anything like it. Flo Kennedy, the late feminist advocate and lawyer, who was seated in the courtroom, said she'd never seen anything like it, either. We were in a celebratory mood when we left the courtroom and some of the blacks in the audience came up and congratulated me. The two cops were obviously angry. They had their guns and their other toys, but I had the words and I had beaten them with the words.

This experience, though time-consuming, was worth more than a year at a university. It taught me how I stand as a black man in the United States. Whites have their government, with its three branches and innumerable services. The police are my government. They can regulate my comings and goings with all of the leeway accorded modern-day patrollers, which they are. They can request an I.D. check with or without cause. They can invade my home without a warrant and the criminal justice system will tolerate this invasion with a wink and a nod. They can arrest me without cause, judge me, and in some cases carry out the sentence. Sometimes they decide that the penalty is death. And though some black males and feminists are still engaged in a print fight, these cops have never heard of a gender war; they shoot black women as well as black men. Though black men are still the No. 1 public enemy of many white Americans, black women are becoming a growing part of the prison population. My experience with the New York police taught me that the Bill of Rights doesn't apply to me. When Calvin, Duncan, and I were marched into the Lower East Side precinct, I said, in my foolishness, "Thomas Jefferson wouldn't approve of this." A detective who was passing by said, "Fuck Thomas Jefferson." How right he was. Most whites enjoy their "rights." The rest of us live in a police state, a crude backward nation within this great democracy, presided over by primitives like Officer Shrunk. He could violate my "rights" not only if I were an ordinary person, but even if I were a celebrity football player beloved by millions. He could plant evidence on me and if I were of little material wealth he could force me to plea bargain for a crime I didn't commit and if I did have some means to hire a lawyer, he could get up in the stand and testilie his ass off.

When I left New York, I was no longer the innocent idealist I was when I entered New York in 1962. I knew a thing or two. But if my most serious encounter with the New York police was bizarre, an encounter with the Los Angeles police was even more bizarre.

In the summer of 1967, a few months before the publication of my first novel, I moved to Los Angeles. During the week, I worked on my second novel, *Yellow Back Radio Broke-Down*, a hip takeoff on the old western novels called yellow backs, from which the cowboys derived their style. These books were usually written by dudes from the East like me. It took me a while to adjust to the automobile culture of California and I didn't get a driver's license until the early seventies. One day, I was nearly arrested for walking while black.

It had been my custom to walk to the downtown Los Angeles library to do the research that would go into the writing of the novel. One day, I was passing through a black neighborhood when a police car pulled up and some police in plainclothes piled out of their car. They rushed up to me and snatched the pouch in which I carried my notes and books. A crowd of African-Americans who had gathered began to laugh when they removed the contents from the pouch—some books and a notebook. The police said they thought that it was a lady's purse that I had stolen. The pouch didn't look anything like a purse.

I said, for the crowd to hear, "Gee, you can't even go to the library anymore." The cops were humorless though, and piled back into their car and sped off. Now that I look back upon it, I could have been beaten or shot for acting smart. When I first arrived in New York, I was standing on the corner in Greenwich Village, talking to some friends—an act of blacks congregating that was banned by the old Black Codes—and a black policeman told us to move on. I said something clever and I'll never forget the hatred in the black cop's eyes. He banned me from ever returning to Greenwich Village, a demand that I of course ignored. Once in a while, the police will be frank about their true role. One day we were sitting in PeeWee's, a bar that was on Avenue A on the Lower East Side, and the police came bursting in, guns drawn. When they found that no crime had been committed or that there was no disturbance, one of them said. "We just wanted to be ready." Ready for what? To wage an all-out ethnic war against black Americans? No matter how prosperous black Americans become, in the back of their minds is the knowledge of what happened to the Indians.

My next problem with the police occurred when I was writing my novel *Mumbo Jumbo* in the splendid isolation of the Berkeley Hills, the conservative upper-income area unseen by those who think of radicalism when they think of Berkeley, California. I decided to buy a car. I knew nothing about cars. I noticed an unassuming plain used black sedan for sale on the lot. It cost $1,400. It turned out to be a Humber Super Snipe, a British car with a Rolls Royce engine. Inside, it was finished with luxurious red leather. Frequently, when I drove the car, the police who wanted to know whether the car belonged to me stopped me. One said he stopped me because he wanted to look at the engine. Liar.

For the next few years my encounters with the police were minor. I'd get followed sometimes when going to work at the university, especially when a black criminal had committed some crime and was at large. This happens frequently. All black men come under suspicion when the police are after one, usually when the person has committed an offense against a white. A typical incident happened a few years ago when I was seated in a restaurant. A police car drove up and the occupants, a white girl and the police, stared at me for about thirty seconds. I said nothing about it to my dinner companions, and the policeman and the white girl drove away. All the time, I was trying to reconstruct my whereabouts for the previous week. Just in case.

In 1983, while I was producing a television version of my play *Mother Hubbard*, I had dropped off Jason Buzas, a New York director whom I had sent for to direct the play. As I drove down Shattuck Avenue in Berkeley I was stopped by the Berkeley police, who came down on me, red lights whirling, like gangbusters. They checked out my registration and told me that they had stopped me because a robbery had been committed. I was tired and told them that I didn't feel like robbing anything. When they discovered that I worked at the University of California at Berkeley, they got nervous. One of them said that they had stopped me because I'd been drinking. They were trying to get their lies straight. I was a teetotaler then and I've been one ever since.

My next encounter with the police occurred after Kofi Natambu, the poet and Malcolm X biographer, invited me down to the California Institute of Arts in April 1991 to give a lecture. We had left the Burbank airport and were walking in the parking lot when three plainclothes white men approached us. They identified themselves as members of the Airport Narcotics Security something or other. They wanted to know why I had used an exit different from the one used by the other Southwest passengers. I didn't have any baggage and so I used the main exit, while the passengers with bags used a different exit. The officers were very tense. On Terry Gross's NPR show, *Fresh Air,* I had heard one of the many white experts of black things say that the police only hassled the black underclass. I thought of this when I identified myself as a professor at the University of California at Berkeley who was down for a lecture. They really lit into me then. They asked me to produce a ticket, which I did. I figured that if I exercised my rights and refused I would have been arrested and my briefcase planted with narcotics so that they could make a charge. Many whites believe that blacks are crazy when they accuse the police of planting evidence. These whites are the ones who are crazy, coddled by the criminal justice system and bewitched by the media into believing that American crime is black or brown when over 70 percent of arrests in both cities and rural areas are of whites. In fact, according to recent FBI statistics, it is white adult crime that's on the increase. Many whites are programmed and manipulated by politicians who pay for intellectuals and op-eds written at the service of think tanks. They are seduced by an education that traffics in expensive lies. They live in an intellectually and culturally confined world that's similar to the one inhabited by the character in *The Truman Show*.

At the turn of the century, Booker T. Washington complained

that the media emphasized the "weaknesses" of African-Americans. According to Barry Glassner, things haven't changed. In his book, *The Culture of Fear*, Glassner criticizes the media for stigmatizing black men. "Thanks to the profuse coverage of violent crime on local TV news programs, night after night, black men rob, rape, loot, and pillage in the living room." The media does its part in influencing the attitudes of the white public, keeping white pathology a secret and serving as a sort of public relations annex for the police, so that warlike measures against the black people by the police are tolerated. The media have modern sophisticated tools that Joseph Goebbels would envy.

I've only had one police incident since the one at the Burbank airport. It was as bizarre as the others. I appeared on *Nightline* in a discussion of police brutality and said that one cure would be for police to live in the communities they served. The next day, I pulled up in front of the Bank of America at Lake Merritt in Oakland and was immediately accosted by the searching eyes of a policeman. I figured he had seen the program and was about to provoke an incident. I was right. As I got out of the car, I put on my am/fm earphones. He came up and told me that it was illegal to wear earphones while driving a car. I hadn't been wearing them while driving a car. He was just trying to start something. I said, "Thank you, officer, for informing me of that." I figured that I would have the last word, as I have had on all of the other policemen with whom I have had an unpleasant incident. I had run into Officer Shrunk and his partner in New York, a few months after my case had gone to trial. When they saw me they managed some weak idiotic smirks. I filed away their smirks, because I knew that I would have the last word.

The police wouldn't be able to wage war against the black population without the collusion of the majority of whites. In criticizing the growing prison industry that treats blacks as merchandise just as they were in slavery, Jerome G. Miller wrote in his book, *Search and Destroy*: "To the inner cities, all this criminal activity brought a war mentality, destructive strategies, and vicious tactics, which exacerbated the violence and fueled social disorganization far beyond whatever negative effects might hitherto have been attributed to single-parent homes, welfare dependency, or the putative loss of family values. The white majority embraced the draconian measures with enthusiasm, particularly as it became clear that they were falling heaviest on minorities in general, and on African-American males in particular."

Ken Auletta, author of a "tough-love" book entitled *Underclass,* said that the complaints of black motorists that they have been subjected to racial profiling by the New Jersey police were exercises in P.C. If Auletta and other public intellectuals believe that blacks are P.C.-ing or making up things, he can do more than dismiss such complaints with an imperious back of the hand. He can do the Griffin-Solomon test. Both were white men who altered their features and lived as black men. With advances in makeup art, Auletta can test his theory about P.C. without undergoing the chemical injection that was required of Griffin. It wouldn't be too much for Auletta to make such a transformation. He's already dark. Maybe he would come to different conclusions from those of Griffin and Solomon. Griffin said he experienced a hostility that he didn't suffer as a white man. Solomon, a student, abandoned the experiment. He couldn't take it. This might be an idea for a new *Survivor* show. All of the columnists and op-eders who accuse blacks of P.C.-ing can live as blacks. See how many survive.

The majority of whites endorse the Gestapo tactics of the police as long as it keeps black people out of their hair. Notice how the media glorifies Mark Fuhrman, the policeman who was caught lying during the O. J. Simpson case, a man who said that "the only good nigger is a dead nigger." The support for the presidential candidacy of General Colin Powell, according to one right-wing pundit, was based upon his ability to handle "crime" and " welfare," which in the American vocabulary are synonyms for "nigger." Colin Powell directed the National Guard in its invasion of Los Angeles after the Rodney King riots. If the "gangs" hadn't retreated, I'm sure that this man, who tried to cover up the My Lai Massacre, would have pulled a Republican Guard number on these gangs. Whites want Colin Powell to be the head Overseer for black Americans. Ronald Reagan was elected and David Duke received a large percentage of white votes in Louisiana because both promised to put blacks back in their places.

An indication of how little most whites care about how the blacks and browns are treated by the police comes from a poll about police brutality taken after an incident when a New York policeman sodomized a Haitian-American citizen with a toilet plunger. Most blacks and Hispanics felt that police brutality was a problem. Most whites didn't. (When NBC broadcast this poll, it left out the fact that Hispanics agreed with blacks—a way of isolating the black population as malcontents and paranoids who are devoted to political correctness.)

Randall Kennedy and other members of the Talented Tenth might argue that African-Americans are under scrutiny because the crime rate among blacks is so high. But neither Kennedy nor Orlando Patterson, who also believes that the problems of millions of blacks are self-induced, can explain why other ethnic groups are targets of the police. In Northern California, an Asian-American was recently shot to death by the police because, according to them, he was threatening them with martial arts moves. A Hispanic man, caught in the border wars now being waged against Hispanics and Indians in the Southwest, described his ordeal, which resulted from being stopped by the border police, on Pacifica Radio News. He was stopped at 9 p.m. and when he told the officer that he was the town's former mayor, they said, "that don't cut no ice with us." It didn't cut no ice with them because they knew that in the eyes of the Anglo population, they had more power than a Hispanic mayor.

On October, 22, 1998, the National Council of La Raza issued a news release complaining about police brutality aimed at Hispanics. "Groups ranging from Amnesty International to the Mexican

American Bar Association to the Human Rights Watch have documented countless incidents of law enforcement abuse and excessive use of force. It is insulting, therefore to be told nothing is wrong when you have case after case [of] police officers not being charged and instead set loose back on the streets." Here again, the legion of writers who get paid by places like the *New York Times*, the *New Yorker*, the *New Republic*, and *Atlantic Monthly* to coast along on the familiar cliches about race and crime show their incompetence in analyzing such issues as police brutality. It's not single-parent households that get you into trouble with the law enforcement; Hispanics are often praised by the same writers for their strong family ties. It's your black or brown skin that marks you like the Star of David and the pink triangle marked Jews and gays in Nazi Germany. The Harvard Talented Tenth should get out of Cambridge from time to time and learn what's happening in this country.

Though the Harvard Talented Tenth believe that they have more in common with their upper-class colleagues than with other blacks, if the American government decided to exterminate blacks as they did the Indians, or to put them in concentration camps as they did the Japanese-Americans, or deport them as they did Mexican-Americans, the Tenth's white Harvard colleagues would sever ties with them. Wouldn't know them. Probably testify against them. Turn them in.

From the very beginning, when Africans were stored on ship prisons and were held in jail, innocent of any crime, while waiting to be sold, prison has been a second home for blacks and a home away from home. Even Clarence Thomas, a conservative, when watching a prison bus full of black prisoners said "there but for the grace of God go I," because he knows that he can be injured by a policeman for whom all blacks are the same. Even Talcott, the right-wing black protagonist who wanders through the novel *The Emperor of Ocean Park,* dismissing left-wing characters with terms like "pig-headed" and who disdains P.C., fears a false arrest; he said, ". . . and I experience, briefly, the secret fear of false arrest that every black male in America nurtures somewhere deep within." The powerful and the powerless. The police and their enablers, the courts and the prosecutors, even put powerful black politicians under surveillance. Maybe if the secret government had spent as much time tracking al-Qaeda as it did prying into the personal lives of black politicians and leaders, the disasters of 9/11 could have been avoided. Recently the police detained the son of Detroit's mayor and a few years ago, the son of Earl Graves, publisher of *Black Enterprise* magazine. In the late 1990s, some psychotic New Jersey police held a famous African-American dancer to the ground, until they saw that he was on the cover of that week's *Time* magazine.

Whites often justify their actions against blacks by pointing to the fear that whites have of blacks. Police shoot blacks because blacks live in "tough" neighborhoods and the police are afraid and don't know what to expect of blacks. This fear of blacks is whipped up by the media, and an industry of rabid-mouth op-eders, talk-show hosts, think tank wonks, and any number of fallen intellectuals out to make a quick buck. As the Asian-American and Hispanic populations grow and the media find it impossible to ignore these groups, the fear of blacks will also become the fear of Asian-Americans and Hispanics. Admiration for the model minority can turn to hatred overnight in a white America that is constantly kept in a state of mobilization against the Other by politicians and journalists. One minute many whites were loving the Chinese for the movie *Crouching Tiger Hidden Dragon*; the next minute they were telling the talk show demagogues that they wanted the Chinese-Americans interred. This came after members of an American spy plane were detained by China. Shortly afterward, a movie entitled *Pearl Harbor* was released. This time Japanese-Americans received threats from those whites who were inflamed by the movie.

The author William Wong singled out NBC's Tim Russert as one who did not challenge anti-Chinese remarks made by a guest.

Russert works the white-resentment-against-blacks hustle as well. He's not just another journalist. Russert is a high executive at NBC news. He constantly cites the statistic that seven out of ten African-American households are headed by single mothers, yet ignores statistics that show a dramatic plunge in out-of-wedlock births among African-American women. Nor does Russert ever mention that "out-of-wedlock" births among white women are shooting upward. His hero is Senator Daniel Moynihan, who used the term "speciation" when referring to the birth rate among black women and, according to the Watergate Papers, shamelessly solicited the job as "underclass" overseer from President Richard Nixon. Moynihan has made a profession of assigning to blacks stereotypes that once were floated about Irish, perhaps as a way of gaining admission to the "white" club of New York intellectuals.

Whites have been betrayed by their white supremacist education and their leaders, and they have been indoctrinated by the media. Most of them have no idea how to deal in a United States in which they are no longer the majority, and their leaders aren't preparing them for it. I was not surprised by a census report that whites, more than any other group, are most likely to live among themselves, yet professional black-baiters like David Horowitz are always calling blacks separatists. James Lowen, in his forthcoming book, *White Towns,* writes about towns that were established to not only exclude blacks, but also Chinese-Americans, the model minority. Minister Louis Farrakhan is the media's idea of a separatist and a cottage industry has grown up around attacking him as such. Yet, there are probably more whites living within a twenty-five-mile radius of Minster Farrakhan than blacks and Latinos living within a twenty-five-mile radius of many whites, who are beginning to live in white enclaves like Santa Fe, New Mexico, where Latinos are being driven from their traditional homelands. Besides, Minster Farrakhan is a concert violinist who probably knows more about European culture than average whites kept in the dark ages by the monoculturalists who provide them with information and education.

Booker T. Washington and Marcus Garvey were right. The majority of whites will never integrate. They will continue to vote for pro-white candidates even if these candidates advocate measures that lead to the poisoning of their water and food. And since most whites and the white men with guns who protect them can't tell dark people apart, the harassment inflicted upon blacks for hundreds of years will be aimed at the new immigrants. An attorney from the Middle East told me that he was subjected to racial profiling by the Maryland police, and Indians from the subcontinent are complaining about white Californians referring to them as "niggers." The former chancellor of the University of California, a Chinese-American, was accosted on the streets of Berkeley—recently found to be the whitest city in the country—by a man who told him to go back to China. (Hate crimes against Jews and Arabs in Berkeley have quadrupled since 9/11. Some Berkeley residents, and organizations like the Bay Area chapter of the American Arab Anti-Discrimination Committee, have become so alarmed over this increase that they proposed hate crime legislation to the Berkeley City Council on May 28, 2002.)

As I was winding up this essay, I had one of those encounters that black men have to deal with too often. I went on an errand to Oakland's downtown Civic Center. When I returned to the garage to get my car, I got off on the wrong floor. I was wandering about, trying to find my car, an activity that goes on throughout the United States each day. A white woman walked toward me. When she saw me she hesitated, a scene that occurs throughout the United States each day when a black man and a white woman are alone in a public space. I ignored her and kept searching for my car. While walking through one aisle, I noticed her at the other end of the garage. She was staring across the garage at me. It was the kind of stare of terror and hate that's gotten thousands of black men incarcerated, maimed, or lynched and whole sections of the Black Belts wiped out and their inhabitants massacred.

Pampered ex-suburban women, who saw their first black person when they joined the Student Nonviolent Coordinating Committee or moved into Greenwich Village, are saying that gender trumps race as the most serious social problem. The Talented Tenthers who, like their inspiration, W. E. B. DuBois, seldom leave a college campus, are saying that it's class.

But in an everyday situation like the parking garage, a white woman has more power than a black woman or a black male millionaire. When I came down another aisle, confused because I wasn't aware that I was on a different floor from the one where I had parked my car, I noticed a white man, whose job was apparently that of filling the cars on this floor with gas. He was standing, frozen, glaring at me. His fists were clenched. He had deputized himself as a patroller. He was ready.

Suddenly a security guard approached me and demanded that I produce a ticket. He had been watching me on video. (I guess they sent a Hispanic guard, so that if I were a really dangerous black man and I harmed him, it would be no big deal.) I told him that I had left it in the car. He said that it was probably upstairs. He escorted me upstairs and followed me until I located the car. Unlike those kids at the movie who were disturbed by the Phantom Menace, I took the incident in stride. I was a veteran and this was another day at the front.

—An earlier version of this article
appeared in *Police Brutality*,
edited by Jill Nelson, 2000

CHAPTER 5

Booker Versus the Negro-Saxons

WRITTEN IN A MODERN READER-FRIENDLY PROSE STYLE, *Up From Slavery*, by Booker T. Washington, chronicles his rise from a nameless slave child to a man who was treated as though he were the president of a sovereign nation. Not only does his life provide a valuable glimpse into the state of race relations between the end of the Civil War and 1915, the year of his death, but it also shows how his strategies for the advancement of African-Americans and those of his chief rival, W. E. B. DuBois, sometimes collided but often complemented each other. For example, the National Negro Business League, of which Booker T. Washington was president, was W. E. B. DuBois's idea.

The result of the two men's efforts was the development of Tuskegee Institute which, since beginning with an enrollment of thirty students, has graduated thousands of professionals, and the founding of the National Association for the Advancement of Colored People. The N.A.A.C.P's use of legal challenges to advance the cause of African-Americans has been enormously successful. Ironically, however, the organization drew some of the same criticism from sixties' militants that was formerly aimed at Booker T. Washington by turn-of-the-century firebrands like

Monroe Trotter, a Harvard graduate and editor of the newspaper, *Guardian*.

So vehemently opposed to Washington's policies was Trotter that he participated in a rowdy Boston event arranged to disrupt Washington's appearance at the Columbus Avenue Zion Church in the summer of 1903. This disturbance became known as the Boston Riot. Using Monroe Trotter's serving of a thirty-day sentence for his participation as a symbol of martyrdom, the riot was one of those events that inspired the Niagara Movement, named for members of the African-American elite who met at the Erie Beach Hotel in Ontario, Canada, later the same year. They met to form "organized determination and aggressive action on the part of men who believe in Negro freedom and growth."

Washington was right to ask whether Trotter and his friends would have pulled such a stunt in a white church and he found it ironic that the Talented Tenth, which accused the "Tuskegee Machine," Washington's center for dispensing rewards to friends and punishment to foes, of suppressing dissent, would, in this instance, seek to prohibit his free speech.

In 1903, DuBois defined the Talented Tenth:

> Can the masses of the Negro people be in any possible way more quickly raised than by the effort and example of this aristocracy of talent and character? Was there ever a nation on God's fair earth civilized from the bottom upward? Never; it is, ever was and ever will be from the top downward that culture filters. The Talented Tenth rises and pulls all that are worth the saving up to their vantage ground. This is the history of human progress; and the two historic mistakes which have hindered that progress were the thinking first that no more could ever rise save the few already risen; or second, that it would better the unrisen to pull the risen down.

But Trotter's action only reflected the frustration of Northern elitist intellectuals, Negro-Saxons, with Booker T. Washington's policies, which they viewed as insuring the inferior position of African-Americans in the United States. Their criticisms dogged Washington throughout his career. DuBois even blamed Washington for the Jim Crow laws that Southern states adopted following Washington's Atlanta Compromise Speech, which called for social separation of the races.

In some ways this was a conflict about class. Washington was born a slave and did not receive "higher education," while some of his enemies were born free and were Harvard educated. Washington was also correct when he characterized the difference between W. E. B. DuBois and himself as one of appealing to different constituencies. In a letter to Emmett Jay Scott, his trusted aide, Washington said, "the Negroes of the South are with me . . . and only the 'intellectuals' of the North are against me." He also criticized DuBois for living in the North and only visiting the South to promote trouble between African-Americans and whites.

DuBois did spend thirteen years on the campus of Atlanta University, but, according to his autobiography, rarely ventured from the campus. In 1911, Washington wrote, "Dr. DuBois pursues the policy of stirring up strife between white people and black people. This would not be so bad, if after stirring up strife between white and black people in the South, he would live in the South and be brave enough to face conditions which his unwise course has helped to bring about; but instead of doing that he flees to the North and leaves the rank and file of colored people in the South no better off because of the unwise course which he and others like him have pursued."

Washington also criticized DuBois for being manipulated by whites. In a letter to Washington from his aide, Thomas Fortune, written in 1911, after attending a New York meeting during which, according to Fortune, DuBois addressed "longhairs" and "discontents," Fortune agreed with Washington that DuBois was "allowing himself to be used to put race leadership in the hands of white men."

Maybe the Negroes of the South sympathized with Washington because they had first-hand experience with the particularly cruel, genocidal, and macabre (the bodies of lynching victims were carved up and used as souvenirs) style of racism that he was up against, while his critics were treated in the same manner that the French and other Europeans treated talented colored expatriates before droves of coloreds began pouring into their countries.

Washington was a practical man. *Up From Slavery* is full of practical advice about everything from growing vegetables to selling bricks. His controversial speech, delivered at the Cotton States and International Exposition in 1895, held in Atlanta, is a masterpiece of hard-line practicality. It has become known as "The Atlanta Compromise Speech." Washington knew that in order to win over the confidence of white supporters he had to pacify the primal fear of many Southern white men. He knew that although a Southern white man could help himself to black women, the way white fathers exploited his and Frederick Douglass's African mothers, that white men, like novelist Thomas Dixon, became psychotic at the idea of black men and white women intermingling. This is what integration meant to these primitives—white women making themselves available to black men. The line in the speech that gained the biggest applause of that day, not only from white men but from white women—"The fairest women of Georgia stood and cheered"—dealt with social separation. He said, "In all things that are purely social we can be as separate as the fingers." From the time of the arrival of African men in this hemisphere to this day, white men have used the threat of sexual liaisons between black men and white women in order to gain more political and financial power and to murder thousands of black men.

In her book *White Women, Black Men: Illicit Sex in the 19th Century South*, Martha Hodes writes, "black men's hopes for and insistence on equality brought public expressions of fear from white Southerners, and those fears included direct references to white women and sex." For their part, many white women have used the threat of the black rapist to torment, taunt, and blackmail white

men emotionally. In her book, *Mothers of Invention*, Drew Gilpin
Faust notes the sign on a float bearing young white girls in a turn-of-
the-century parade. It read "Protect Us" and the parade was staged
to support a candidate committed to black disenfranchisement.

Booker T. Washington met this hot-button issue head on, and
by doing so bought some time for black economic development.
His stance would be met by charges of cowardice by Northern critics who invoked the names of black rebels Denmark Vesey and Nat
Turner. None of these elitists, however, had ever participated in an
armed revolt. Nor had their white patrons. Though lynching still
occurred, future historians may credit Washington with forestalling
an even greater disaster, the extermination of Southern black people by those who had proven that they were capable of such ethnic
cleansing. In one speech, Washington showed his awareness of the
Fort Pillow massacre, during which a mad man named General
Nathan Bedford Forrest, a Confederate general, and founder of the
Ku Klux Klan, massacred black men, women, and children even
though they had surrendered. He knew what had happened to the
Cherokee who tried their best to assimilate and adopt the white
man's ways, only to be removed from their homelands and sent on
a Trail of Tears ordered by Andrew Jackson. His experience with
Native Americans at Hampton Institute gave him a first-hand
glimpse of how whites handled warriors.

Even to this day, the homicide rate among white Southern men
is higher than that among Northern white men. These are the people who after the Civil War sought economic opportunities in the
West. Their savagery alarmed even the Rough Rider Theodore Roosevelt, who noted, "Many of the frontiersmen are brutal, reckless,
and overbearing." These are the people who gave us Jesse James,
Frank James, and the Younger family, and their leader, William C.
Quantrill. A Civil War historian, Kenneth C. Davis, describes these
men and others like them as " cold-blooded" and "psychotic."

In an article entitled "Southern Curse; Why America's Murder
Rate Is So High," published in the *New York Times*, Fox Butterfield

quoted historian David Hackett Fischer, who offered an explana-
tion for "Southern bellicosity." Fischer, a professor at Brandeis University, said, "a critical factor was the heavy settlement of the South
by immigrants referred to today as Scotch Irish—people from the
north of Britain, the lowlands of Scotland and the north of Ireland.
These settlers, whom Benjamin Franklin described as 'white savages,' brought with them a culture based upon centuries of fighting
between the kings of England and Scotland over the borderlands
they inhabited. They had a penchant for family feuds, a love of
whisky and a warrior ethnic that demanded vengeance."

The masses of Southern black people knew what Washington
was up against. Though one of his more fervent critics accused him
of designing a program that "practically accepts the alleged inferiority of the Negro races," passages in *Up From Slavery* gush with
racial pride. "From any point of view, I had rather be what I am, a
member of the Negro race, than be able to claim membership with
the most favored of any other race." Washington referred to the
African-American race as "the race to which I am proud to belong."
By contrast, his Harvard tormentors seemed uncomfortable with
their African heritage. W. E. B. DuBois, a product of a white supremacist curriculum, believed that whites were an advanced race
and that African societies were primitive, a view that would be considered uninformed by those who have examined African literature,
art, dance, and mathematics. DuBois also characterized the masses
of African-Americans as "primitive" and pinned his hopes for
African-American progress on a Talented Tenth, one tenth of the
10 million population of African-Americans at the time, an elite
that would lead African-Americans to liberation.

Early in the reading of *Up From Slavery*, one realizes the difference between Booker T. Washington and his critics, who were referred to in one letter as "academic theorists." While the critics monitored and were inspired by the theories of a succession of white
thinkers, Booker T. Washington based his actions not on books but
on experience. DuBois, Ralph Ellison, and their intellectual follow-

ers believed that if one digested the contents of "Great Books," that is, books written by white men, one would be, in DuBois's words, "wedded" to the truth. They believed that by ingesting this material, African-Americans would assimilate "high," that is, European, culture. Their obedience to this concept led them to accept uncritically material that was not based upon science but often on folklore and wild speculation. While Booker T. Washington based his values on the teachings of Christianity, his critics worshipped at the altar of modernism, a movement now considered passe.

Unlike the modernists, Washington relied upon common sense, and experience. His mother, Jane, a resourceful women who deserves a separate biography, taught him the frugality that would lead to his running Tuskegee the way that a banker would run a bank. She showed him how to avoid spending money on foolish things. He had visited homes where only one fork was available at mealtime, while expensive clocks and organs went unused in the living rooms. The ex-slaves lacked knowledge of fiscal management because they were used to being property while others looked after the books.

After working in the household of Mrs. Viola Ruffner, a "strict Yankee," and apparent housekeeper from hell, Washington said, "the lessons that I learned in the home of Mrs. Ruffner were as valuable to me as any education." He didn't study the conditions of the post-slavery generation through sociological works, but lived among them, and his ideas about education were formed by what he observed. When he used the image of "a lone black boy poring over a French grammar amid the weeds and dirt of a neglected home" he knew what he was talking about. His writings are full of anecdotes about blacks who knew abstract theories but didn't know how to raise vegetables or maintain a house. Booker T. Washington learned by observation and these early lessons would inform his conduct for the rest of his life. Surrounded by filth in his early years, he became obsessively devoted to hygiene and other forms of cleanliness. Washington made much of the importance of the toothbrush, which for him became "the gospel of the tooth-brush."

Also part of that gospel was the insistence on "absolute cleanness of the body."

W. E. B. DuBois asked what Socrates and Saint Francis of Assisi would say to Washington's point about ex-slaves who knew the classics but had no knowledge of how to fend for themselves, a remark that would prompt a practical man like Washington to refer to DuBois as a "dunce." When Washington described a black intellectual as someone with "high hat, imitation gold eye-glasses, a showy walking-stick, kid gloves, fancy boots, and what not," we have a pretty good idea whom he is signifying upon. The men exchanged insults and at one point DuBois referred to Washington as the Arch Tempter, and synonym for Satan. Sometimes, his anger with Washington led him to abandon the scientific objectivity that he admired. His charge that Washington had bribed the black press was unsubstantiated and he was not above printing tabloid-styled gossip about Thomas Fortune, one of the members of Washington's "Tuskegee Machine," a derogatory name given to Washington's organization by his enemies. (DuBois's autobiography hints at his own bout with sex addiction.) It is also clear that the Tuskegee Machine, often in a competition with DuBois and his followers for white patrons, frustrated some of DuBois's career goals.

Though commentators dwell on the feud between Washington and the African-American New England intellectuals as one over Washington's insistence that industrial education for African-Americans take priority over what he considered the frills of the "New England" curriculum, Washington was not inflexible on this point. DuBois admitted this in his autobiography, a book that, in some ways, is superior to *The Souls of Black Folk*. In a letter commemorating the career of his patron, General Samuel Chapman Armstrong, Washington endorses both "hand" and "head" education, that half of the student's education be devoted to learning industrial trades and half to book learning. Washington also complained to the editor of the *Indianapolis Star* about DuBois's distorting his record. "He knows perfectly well I am not seeking to confine the Negro race to industrial education nor make them hewers of wood and drawers of water, but I am trying to do the same thing for the Negro which is done for all races of the world, and that is to make the masses of them to combine brains with hand work to the extent that their services will be wanted in the communities where they live, and thus prevent them from becoming a burden and a menace."

DuBois's attitude toward Washington was inconsistent. At first, he endorsed Washington's Atlanta Compromise Speech, but he later denounced it in his book *The Souls of Black Folk* (possibly in an attempt to woo Washington's white patrons; he succeeded). He then accepted some of Washington's programs in 1909, but later resigned from the integrationist N.A.A.C.P for advocating a limited form of segregation for blacks.

Washington, as revealed in *Up From Slavery*, was consistent. Focused. His main goal was the growth and sustenance of Tuskegee Institute, micro-managing every detail of the operation. A group of photos that appear in a report by Washington entitled, "Twenty-Five Years Of Tuskegee, The Building Up of the Negro as Shown by the Growth and Work of this School Managed Wholly by Negroes," tells the story. The photographs show the rise of Tuskegee from a few shack-like buildings to a building with Greek columns twenty-five years later. There are photos of African-American students running a high-speed machine, testing milk, working in a harness shop, in a sewing class. Photographs in a 1903 report entitled "The Successful Training Of The Negro" show students building the foundation for the C. P. Huntington Memorial Building and the girl's dormitory, building roads, and attending repair, carpentry, blacksmithing, shoe-making, dressmaking, and tailoring shops. Students are shown printing the school paper and attending a class in mechanical drawing. Tuskegee opened on July 4, 1881, with one teacher and thirty pupils. Twenty-five years later, it comprised eighty-three buildings, 22,000 acres of land, and an endowment of $1,275,664.

So successful have DuBois's followers and their intellectual descendants been in defining Booker T. Washington's reputation that he has been characterized by many as an accommodationist and worse. A more careful examination of the educator's career reveals that Washington was more complicated than his critics would have us believe. As Louis R. Harlan said, "by private action [Booker T. Washington] fought lynching, disenfranchisement, peonage, educational discrimination, and segregation."

DuBois and his supporters would later accuse Washington of appeasing whites, but one could argue that DuBois had to bend to the pressure of whites more than Washington did. Indeed there is evidence that DuBois, when attacking Washington, sometimes did the bidding of whites who believed that they should be the arbiters of who should be the political, cultural, and intellectual leaders of black Americans, an arrogant attitude that exists to this day. When Booker T. Washington traveled to Europe, John Mulholland put DuBois up to attacking Washington in an "Appeal to England and Europe," undermining Washington's visit and accusing him of painting too rosy a picture of American race relations. Like the creators of black Divas and Divuses today, some of the white N.A.A.C.P. directors were hypocrites too. Oswald Villard, a white philanthropist and board member of the N.A.A.C.P., this organization devoted to integration, refused to socialize with DuBois. "He had married a wife from Georgia, a former slave state, and consequently I could never step foot in his house as a guest, nor could any other of his colored associates," DuBois said in his autobiography, a book ignored by the DuBois cult.

While the 1960s may have belonged to W. E. B DuBois, the 1990s were definitely Bookerite. DuBois had criticized Washington for turning away from politics in favor of economic development. This turning away from politics toward economic development and self-sufficiency seems to be the trend among a growing African-American middle class, who've found that electing mayors and other officials to government hasn't changed the lives of the masses of African-Americans. In a speech made before the Union League Club of Brooklyn on February 12, 1896, over 100 years ago, Washington said, "We have spent time and money making political stump speeches and in attending political conventions, that could better have been spent starting a dairy farm, or a truck garden, and thus have laid a material foundation on which we could have stood and demanded our rights." In a number of manifestos, articles, and op-ed pieces, African-Americans are announcing that political power without economic power is meaningless.

Separatism and entrepreneurship seem to have captured the imagination of the Hip Hoppers like Sister Souljah. Spike Lee, also. His contracts include Nike, a sneakers manufacturing concern, and the United States Navy, and his film *Jungle Fever*, a tract that warns against race-mixing, was the cinematic version of Washington's "separate in all things purely social." Even the Highlander Center, in Tennessee, which boasts of having trained Rosa Parks and others in civil rights strategies, is now emphasizing economic justice. When asked by a Pacifica radio interviewer her assessment of the future of activism, black economist Julianne Malveaux said that activism would take the form of "economic activism" and "economic boycotts." She mentioned putting pressure on the Fortune 500 to hire more blacks and called for blacks to invest in the system, even though she described herself as anti-capitalist. Jesse Jackson, who, as a young man, was campaigning in the South for the black right to vote, by 1999 was challenging Wall Street, accompanying President Clinton to areas that had missed the economic good times, and urging corporate investment in these areas.

Many blacks have decided that wasting energy on integrating with whites, the majority of whom seem to want to remain separate from everybody, is a useless enterprise. A recent study entitled "Resegregation in American Schools," by Gary Orfield, concluded, "We are clearly in a period when many policymakers, courts, and opinion makers assume that desegregation is no longer necessary." Orlando Patterson, a Harvard sociologist, is the African-American scholar whom the *New York Times* employs to promote its position that the cause of the problems of "the black underclass" is their personal behavior. In July 1999, Patterson responded, in a *Times* op-ed, to the Boston School Committee's decision to end busing. He wrote, "There has been a return to the old Southern doctrine of separate and equal, as long as it is truly equal." Shortly afterward, a poll revealed that young Americans approved of segregation as long as it was equal.

And in what may be the greatest irony of all, an institute named for DuBois has become a center for the creation and promotion of multimillion-dollar cultural products based upon DuBois's ideas. In the manner that it handles its dissidents, "The Tuskegee Machine" of the turn of the century has become "the Harvard Machine" at the end of the century. (Criticism of the Harvard Talented Tenth's now becoming the Princeton Talented Tenth is forbidden in publications that endorse its blame-the-victim comments.) This new Talented Tenth, which blames the black underclass for its problems, is making deals with megacapitalists like Microsoft while the DuBois museum in Accra, Ghana, is running out of resources. Though the Talented Tenth may be DuBoisian in literary style, their leader, Henry Louis Gates Jr., described himself as an " intellectual entrepreneur" during an interview with *Black Issues* magazine. Somewhere, Booker T. is beaming.

How would DuBois feel about such collaboration between his intellectual descendants and an outfit that might be convicted of monopolistic practices? In a speech in Accra, DuBois urged Africans to "boycott the export of big capital from the exploiting world, led by America." Polls show that most blacks are opposed to busing, the technique that liberal reformers believed would bring about Martin Luther King Jr.'s dream. Though Washington's separatist stance angered his elitist critics, the notion of segregation has always appealed to a segment of blacks and has been commodified in recent years (Kwanzaa stamps and X products). Indeed, among younger 1990s African-American intellectuals, segregation is in vogue even though some of its popularizers continue to socialize with whites. So did Washington, for even though he preached social separation he spent a good deal of time in the company of white men and women. He took tea with white women in a segregated railroad car and dined with President Theodore Roosevelt, an event that gave rise in some quarters to the very fears that he sought to calm in his Atlanta Compromise Speech. About the dinner, the *Richmond Times* wrote: "It means that the President is willing that Negroes shall mingle freely with whites in the social circle—that white women may receive attentions from Negro men."

But unlike DuBois, the idealist and visionary (he sincerely believed that Russia was the hope of mankind, that if blacks fought in American wars that whites would respect them, and that white and black workers would unite in common cause), Washington foresaw that segregation would always exist in a country with a white majority, because whites would always insist upon it.

Orlando Patterson, a member of the Harvard Talented Tenth, writing in the *New York Times*, suggested that it was the fault of blacks that integration didn't work. He argued that middle-class whites fled the cities because of the personal behavior of black students, but the personal behavior of black students, or blacks in general for that matter, doesn't explain why whites desire to separate from other groups. White leaders are the ones who passed laws in 1924 excluding Japanese from California (resulting in yet another form of white affirmative action, since one of the motivations behind this measure was to prevent Japanese farmers from competing with white ones). White leaders also backed the exclusion of the Chinese and deportation of Mexican-American citizens and passed resolutions banning the arrival of new people from Mexico. Segregation accompanies some whites wherever they go. Quoted in the *New York Times* of July 12, 1999, Desa Jaconsson, a Native American, complained about the treatment of her people by the white majority in Alaska. "Apartheid is alive and well and it lives in the Arctic, it lives in our schools, and I'm sad to say it lives in the halls of the State legislature." All the way up there near the North Pole! Whites are the ones who are most likely to commit hate crimes against Asian-

Americans, blacks, gays, and others who are different from them. They're the ones who engage in white flight not only from the blacks but from model minorities like Cuban-Americans, who are a power in Miami. Though it's become fashionable among some white authors to blame black separatism for the dissolution of the civil rights movement, whites are the true separatists, and Washington knew it.

Washington was prescient in other matters also. He was a media critic who accused the newspapers of his day of stressing the "weaknesses" of African-Americans. In those days the papers often behaved as lynch mob leaders against African-Americans, a role that the American media haven't abandoned. Newspapers like the *New York Times* attach a black face to all social problems—welfare, crime, drug addiction, AIDS, fatherless households—when these problems can be also found among other ethnic groups and among whites whose flaws are covered up by a media conspiracy of silence. Washington said that the South is the African-American's best friend, a notion that is being echoed by the thousands of African-Americans who are returning to the South after having experienced the racist hatred in the North and the West. After all, though Booker T. Washington was vulnerable to the kind of violence that often came to Southern African-Americans of his stature, it was in the North that he was attacked by a New York mob for being in the wrong neighborhood.

As we enter a new millennium, Booker T. Washington deserves a reassessment unfettered by the bias of Northern elitist African-American intellectuals and comfortable white radicals who would only have been satisfied if Washington had engaged in a wild suicidal shoot-out with whites, who outnumbered the black population three to one, so that they might use his martyr's photo to further their causes. Washington was opposed by those who disagreed with his economic theories. Yet, 100 years later, their's remain untested.

They said that he was soft on lynching, but his statement on lynching, released to Southern newspapers, was forceful and eloquent. They said that he was for the disenfranchisement of black men, yet he opposed disenfranchisement with his personal funds.(They also neglect to mention that when he appeared before the House Committee on Appropriations, in 1894, seeking funds for the Atlanta Exposition, Washington urged that the right of black men to vote not be taken away.) They said that he blamed African-Americans for their problems when, in a strong reply to a black pathology mercenary of the time, an ancestor of the pundits, academics, and intellectuals who've made a career from attacking blacks, he traced African-American antisocial behavior to the institution of slavery, 100 years before editors at the *New York Times* and the *New York Review of Books* were giving credit to the Harvard Talented Tenth for what, in their minds, was a new theory.

Rather than being viewed as an "Uncle Tom," a "coward," and an "accommodationist" (the strangest charge of all since Tuskegee graduates were competitive with whites), Washington should be judged as someone who, despite his shortcomings, rose from humble circumstances to build one of world's centers of learning, literally with his bare hands, and to train thousands of African-Americans in matters of both the hands and the head.

His was more than a Horatio Alger story. Alger's heroes were usually white and free; Washington was black and a slave. That he has been maligned for these many years is not only wrong-headed, but perverse.

Washington was a motivational speaker and a fund-raiser so persuasive that he was able to raise hundreds of thousands of dollars for his school. W. E. B. DuBois was a scholar, a prolific author, a magazine editor, one of the founders of the Pan-African Movement, and a man whose demand for respect led to less humiliation for African-Americans in everyday life.

Instead of Washington and DuBois being pitted against each other, both should be celebrated. What Washington said applied to both:

I have learned that success is to be measured not so much by the position that one has reached in life as by obstacles which he has overcome while trying to succeed. Looked at from this standpoint, I almost reach the conclusion that often the Negro boy's birth and connection with an unpopular race is an advantage, so far as real life is concerned. With few exceptions, the Negro youth must work harder and must perform his tasks even better than a white youth in order to secure recognition. But out of the hard and unusual struggle through which he is compelled to pass, he gets strength, a confidence, that one misses whose pathway is comparatively smooth by reason of birth and race.

A different version of this essay was published as the introduction of Washington's *Up From Slavery,* a Signet Classic

CHAPTER 6

Was W. E. B. DuBois Pro-Nazi?

In his Pulitzer Prize-winning *W. E. B. DuBois, Biography Of a Race*, David Levering Lewis covered the scholar's life from his birth in 1868 to his becoming the editor of the influential magazine, *Crisis*. In an arched, dense prose style, he also wrote about DuBois's beginnings in Great Barrington, Massachusetts, and his education at Fisk, Harvard, and the University of Berlin (now Humboldt University). In addition, DuBois's authorship of important works—*The Suppression of the African Slave Trade, The Souls of Black Folk*—and his teaching chores at the University of Pennsylvania, Wilberforce, and Atlanta University were examined. During this period, DuBois married Nina Gomer, became involved in the Pan-African Movement (a term coined by Henry Sylvester Williams) and the Niagara Movement, organized by Talented Tenth intellectuals to counter the influence of Booker T. Washington, a man identified with compromise and accommodation to segregation by his Northern critics. (Washington accused them of distorting his views; he was right!)

Volume II of *W. E. B. DuBois* is subtitled *The Fight for Equality and the American Century, 1919–1963*. This book covers DuBois's career as the editor of *Crisis*, his bitter feud with Marcus

Garvey, leader of an African colonization and race purity movement, and his continued involvement with the Pan-African Movement. His attitude toward the Harlem Renaissance, the writing of Black Reconstruction, his work with the N.A.A.C.P., and his project *The Encyclopedia of the Negro* are also addressed. Other topics include his struggle with an American government caught up in the anti-Communist hysteria and his eventual repatriation to Ghana. All of these subjects are exhausted with Lewis's devotion to detail and often worshipful regard for the subject, but the parts of the book that will attract the most attention are about DuBois's ambivalent attitude toward Nazi Germany and Imperial Japan. Perhaps it is not surprising that the advocate of the Talented Tenth would find something to admire in dictatorships. After all the Talented Tenth—DuBois's name for an incestuous elite of intellectuals and professionals—were, in Marcus Garvey's words, "unelected." Still are. DuBois's defense of Japan is not surprising since some African-American intellectuals saw the Japanese defeat of the Russian navy in 1905 as a victory of a colored nation over a white one.

The founder of the Talented Tenth comes across in Volume II as a brilliant, arrogant intellectual in constant oscillation between integrationist and segregationist positions. A man who had contentious relationships with both whites and blacks, yet someone capable of putting his ideas to work for the benefit for himself and others. A man of contradictions, criticizing, but then adopting some of the ideas of his foes. And like a true Talented Tenther he, in public, was a devoted feminist, but exhibited patriarchal attitudes toward the women in his private life. (Soothed by the doting he received from Japanese women, he characterized American white women as "impudent and aggressive.") Shakespeare Agamemnon Beard, Harlem Renaissance writer George Schuyler's character, based upon DuBois, had a proclivity for high-yellow secretaries with the least resistance. DuBois was someone who saw himself, in the postwar period, as the spokesperson for "750,000,000" people living under colonial domination and the champion of the world's working class, yet he was a man who lived the life of an aristocrat. He enjoyed rare food, good drink, aristocratic mistresses, and pomp.

But regardless of his weaknesses, his energy was such that he was able to accomplish the work of several lifetimes. A good constitution helped. At the age of seventy DuBois was working a schedule that would exhaust younger men. At the age of ninety-four, he was capable of diving from the high boards at hotel swimming pools and had enough stamina to travel to Asia and Africa. His longevity enabled him to witness the fruits of his inventions as well as take a second look at the positions of some of those with whom he had fought so hard. In the 1960s, when a student, visiting his home in Ghana, made a disparaging remark about DuBois's old nemesis, Booker T. Washington, DuBois defended Washington who, in his day, was treated as though he were Black America's sovereign king. DuBois reminded the youngster of something that his aunt had told him about the sage of Tuskegee, a man who, with the help of his students, built campus buildings with his bare hands. She said, "Don't you forget that that man, unlike you, bears the mark of the lash on his back. He has come out of slavery. . . . You are fighting for the rights here in the North. It's tough, but it's nothing like as tough as what he had to face in his time and his place." DuBois also discovered in Ghana that, while he was the intellect of Pan-Africanism, a program that would bring Africa under African control, Marcus Garvey was its soul. DuBois and his Talented Tenthers waged a relentless and sometimes vicious and indeed racist campaign against Garvey, but Garvey could give as much as he got. He referred to DuBois as an "antebellum Negro" and the Talented Tenth as "octoroons married to octoroons," a remark that revealed the racial and class divisions among African-Americans.

But the main difference between DuBois and his opponents was that DuBois addressed a world audience while his adversaries, like N.A.A.C.P. leaders Walter White and Roy Wilkins, were men obsessed with the day-to-day issues of black survival in the United States. They used the courts to advance the rights of blacks. (Even though these leaders shied away from radical politics, they were red-baited by that cultural warrior, Arthur M. Schlesinger Jr.) His white enemies, many of them academics, were fanatical about maintaining the myth of "white" superiority. In comparison to the suave and worldly DuBois, a pioneer in black studies, whose knowledge of European civilization was superior to most of theirs, these enemies were academic backwoodsmen. During DuBois's trip to Nazi Germany in 1936, on an Oberlaender Fellowship, he observed that a German academic had treated him better than his white colleagues at Chicago, Columbia, and Harvard. (Oberlaender has been identified by Werner Sollors as a Nazi sympathizer who had dined with Hitler.) It was perhaps DuBois's experience in Europe as a young man that gave him an international outlook and his devotion to German culture.

While traveling through Nazi Germany, Lewis wrote, "DuBois's reading of National Socialism ran from equivocal to complimentary. . . . Dictatorship had been unavoidable, had been 'absolutely necessary to put the state in order,' he allowed, after the implosion of the Weimar economy."

"DuBois honored the German War dead and refused to blame Germany for starting the Great War and shared . . . the German outrage at the draconian indemnity imposed by the Allied Powers." Also, DuBois said that "he found National Socialism to be neither 'wholly illogical,' nor 'hypocritical,' but to be still 'a growing and developing body of thought.'" After leaving Germany, DuBois expressed his horror at the treatment of the Jews. He wrote in the *Pittsburgh Courier* that "There has been no tragedy in modern times equal in its awful effects to the fight on the Jews in Germany . . . It is an attack on civilization, comparable only to such horrors as the Spanish Inquisition and the African slave trade. It has set civilization back a hundred years." Nevertheless, some will find his report to the *Pittsburgh Courier* troubling. DuBois wrote that Hitler "showed Germany a way out when most Germans saw nothing but impenetrable mist, and he made the vast majority of Germans believe that his way was the only way." He went on to praise the accomplishments of the regime: "They have domestic peace after a generation of wars and rumors of wars; they have a nation at work, after a nightmare of unemployment."

Clarence Lusane, in his important book, *Hitler's Black Victims: The Historical Experiences of Afro-Germans, European Blacks, Africans and African Americans in the Nazi Era*, reported that DuBois spoke "highly of Hitler's private secretary and party leader, Rudolph Hess." Lusane also took DuBois to task for his observation that German attitudes "did not yet show any trace of racial hatred" toward Afro-Germans, Africans, or others of African descent. The author wrote that "DuBois's love for Germany seems to have blinded or at least clouded his usually sharp reading of racism. . . . While not as observable as the attacks against the Jews, discrimination and racist rhetoric toward Blacks in Germany were occurring." In the late fifties, DuBois complained about being treated like a "nigger" in the United States. Perhaps the VIP treatment accorded his celebrity caused him to ignore the unsavory aspects of the host countries he visited.

After the Cold War began, DuBois, who represented the United States at ceremonies and conferences, experienced persecution from the government he once served. He eventually left the United States for exile in Ghana, but not before delivering a warning. After joining the Communist Party in 1961 he said, "Capitalism cannot reform itself; it is doomed to self-destruction."

Lewis's excellent biography of W. E. B. DuBois, Volume II, reminds us that at one time in this country, opinion wasn't just a plaything, something that could be packaged as entertainment by show-biz "Public Intellectuals." DuBois paid dearly for his defiance, early signs of which could be found in a combative letter he wrote to former President Rutherford B. Hayes after Hayes had made a remark about the intellectual ability of blacks. Like Paul Robeson, DuBois sacrificed wealth for his anti-capitalist positions and would probably be outraged that his name and concepts are being used by an alliance of Talented Tenthers and megacapitalists like Microsoft, AT&T, and Time Warner. And, who knows? DuBois may have the last word. As more evidence emerges that the brand of capitalism that values profits over human life, a capitalism that is waging premeditated murder against the public and the planet, capitalism may one day find itself buried in a shallow grave next to its old enemy, communism. Put there, not by a working class, hopelessly divided by white racism, but by consumers.

—**An earlier version of this article appeared in
the *Village Voice Literary Supplement*,
October/November 2000**

CHAPTER 7

Should Southerners Be Loyal to Scotland, the Confederacy, or the United States?

MANY OF THE MILLIONS AROUND THE WORLD WATCHING AMERICAN television during the turmoil surrounding the return to Cuba of Elian Gonzalez, who had been rescued after his mother died while escaping from Cuba to the United States, may have thought that Florida had been annexed by Cuba, or that Miami had the same relationship with Cuba that South Korea has with North Korea and that China has with Formosa. Northern Cuba. This is because the Cuban flag was ever present as Cuban exiles expressed their views about whether Elian Gonzalez should be reunited with his father in Cuba. Many politicians and public intellectuals waded in on the issue. Some felt that Elian should remain in a "free and democratic" society and others held the opinion that Elian should be reunited with his natural father, even though the father resided in a "Communist country." Some of the callers into *Washington Journal*, the daily United States town meeting of the air that is broadcast over C-Span, were irate at the display of this foreign flag in an American city that has become so Latin it's sometimes called the capital of South America. Well, if the Cuban flag is foreign, the Confederate flag is doubly foreign. It represents a sovereign nation that was established for a brief period in North America. It also represents a nation from which many of the rebels' ancestors migrated.

There's a scene in *The Birth of a Nation,* a film that justifies the actions of the Ku Klux Klan, in which white-hooded murderers surround a banner that reads "Scotland." So attached to Scotland were these rebels that their Confederate flag is a match of the flag of Scotland, and the cross on the flag represents the saltire cross, which represents Scotland in the Union Jack. It also represents the cross of Saint Andrews, the patron saint of Scotland. (Shouldn't some official of the Catholic church step forward to condemn the use of Saint Andrews by a racist terrorist organization?)

So drenched in Celtic culture is the South that author Grady McWhiney, a new secessionist, refers to "Celtic ways in the old South," which, according to Fox Butterfield, writing in the *New York Times*, are responsible for the high Southern homicide rate. Indeed, Kevin Phillips, in *The Cousins' War*, refers to a back–country South Carolina population of Scots-Irish of the 1770s that was devoted to "loose hogs, lewd women, and drunken lay-abouts," something that contemporary Scots-Irish think tank wonks and op-ed columnists might consider when writing yet another article or study that goes after welfare mothers.

Moreover, all of the founders of the Klan were Scots-Irish. It's obvious that the early Scots-Irish wanted to bring Scotland with them when they settled in the South, and some have speculated that though the root of the Civil War was slavery, the war also represented an old European rivalry between the Scots and the English transferred to American soil.

Maybe the Cubans felt it was OK to fly their flag because they'd seen the Southerners fly theirs. Two of theirs. By voting to keep the stars and bars on their state flag, one could argue that Mississippians can't decide whether their loyalty lies with the

United States or with two other sovereign nations, the Confederacy and Scotland. Where are the op-eders who are always condemning African-Americans for encouraging hyphenated Americanism?

Where is the proliferation of national flags going to end? Nathan Hare, author of *The Black Anglo-Saxons*, proposes that the Confederate flag be allowed to fly, if the green, red, and black liberation flag be flown as well. (While visiting Alabama last year, I learned that some enterprising black artists were designing a flag that would blend the Confederate flag with the black liberation flag.)

While the black liberation flag represents the heritage of Marcus Garvey's 1920s Universal Negro Improvement Association, a mass movement that advocated the return of African-Americans to Africa, Southerners argue that the Confederate flag also represents a heritage. A heritage of whipping people?

That being the case, since Florida was once occupied by Spain, why not fly the flag of Spain over the capitol of Florida, as a reminder of Florida's Spanish heritage, or for that matter, the flag of Mexico over Sacramento? And since Louisiana, and cities surrounding the Great Lakes, were once occupied by France, why not the French flag over Detroit? Or the flag of Sweden over Madison, Wisconsin? The Dutch flag over New York City's Gracie Mansion?

Maybe one flag is enough.

CHAPTER 8

John C. Calhoun, Post-Modernist

IT WAS HARD TO READ C-SPAN HOST BRIAN LAMB'S FACE IN January of 2002 as he fielded calls from some Southerners, most of them South Carolinians, who insisted that the flying of the Confederate flag over the state capitol dome was a symbol of the Southern heritage and had nothing to do with slavery. The callers had some answers for the "peculiar institution" of slavery as well. They argued that white workers in sweatshops were worse off than the black slaves and that the Civil War was not fought over slavery, a favorite argument of some white Southern historians who've appeared during C-Span's very useful presidents series. This was also the argument used by a historian who was interviewed in Jefferson Davis's home, the Montgomery White House, yet Robert E. Lee, Alexander H. Stephens, vice president of the Confederacy, Ulysses S. Grant, and Ambrose Bierce, a novelist and a Union officer, all gave slavery as the reason for the war. Other C-Span historians have argued that one could be a slaveowner and be a good man, which might be an argument that the lawyer for the next kidnapper could use when defending his client.

John C. Calhoun, senator from South Carolina and vice president under Andrew Jackson until December 1832, who died in 1850, described himself as a "merciful slaveowner." Indeed, those contemporaries who defend the institution of slavery and the Confederate flag, and who insist that slaveowners were good men, might have been inspired by Calhoun's debating strategies. He was skillful at making institutions that many would regard as evil sound benevolent. He was the original Spin Doctor.

In his introduction to *The Papers Of John C. Calhoun, 1845–1846*, Clyde N. Wilson wrote, "But the negative stereotyping of Calhoun is understandable. He was not only out of step with the main currents of American thought as they later developed, he was also unpopular with both major political elements of his own time." Calhoun may have been out of step with the major political elements of his own time, but his ideas fit not only into the mainstream of contemporary American thought, but into some of the more trendy intellectual circles as well. It would seem that Calhoun has traded in his Colonel Sanders outfit for one from the Gap, no longer the drawling, stock character, Senator Claghorn of the old Fred Allen Show, but chilling in his Soho pad, chuckling, while reading his fellow Scots-Irishman's latest effort to reprove uppity affirmative action blacks, the thinly disguised neoconfederate novel, *A Man In Full*, by Tom Wolfe. In Wolfe's novel, which received lavish coverage from the *New York Times*, one finds the lazy standbys of the Confederate novel, including the black rapist and the incompetent black government, in the city of Atlanta's black administration.

Not only are Calhoun's ideas found in journals like *Southern Partisan*, published by Richard Quinn, but on *Salon.com*, a hip online zine published from San Francisco that seems to find space for every out-of-work, has-been hack writer whose main business is preaching tough love to blacks, exclusively. If Calhoun were around today he would be among the leaders of the new consensus that holds African-American behavior, not racism, responsible for the dire situation in which many blacks find themselves (though those who study the matter, including a "mammoth" survey sponsored by the Russell Sage Foundation, and the Harvard University Multidisciplinary Program in Inequality and Social Policy, conclude that race is still a huge factor). Both W. E. B. DuBois and Booker T. Washington said that a similar consensus was formed among whites in the 1850s.

If, as some African-American intellectuals have argued, there is a trend toward white nationalism, John C. Calhoun was among the first white nationalists. David Duke, a contemporary white nationalist, has founded an organization whose aim is to protect the rights of European-Americans (Duke's ancestors are from Scotland), and arguments by intellectuals like Scots-Irishman Charles Murray, regarding the genetic inferiority of African-Americans, a white nationalist argument that dates to the "Enlightenment," are endorsed by feminists like NPR's Nina Totenberg, who gave Murray's book *The Bell Curve* Olympian praise.

This trend can also be found in cultural criticism. So blatant is the white nationalist mood of the country that over the last year, whites have been credited with inventing art forms that originated among African-Americans. An editor of the *New York Times Magazine*, Gerald Marzorati, reviewed a book about rock and roll without a mention of any of its black pioneers, which is like writing about opera and neglecting to mention Italians.

Calhoun's views about African and African-American culture may sound ignorant to those who know better (especially, the rich who collect African art), but many leading academics and writers agree that Africans and African-Americans have produced no culture. "Never before has the black race of Central Africa, from the dawn of history to the present day, attained a condition so civilized and so improved, not only physically, but morally and intellectually," said Calhoun (the kind of speech that David Horowitz receives millions of dollars from right-wing millionaires to make before naive campus conservatives). The fact that such opinions still exist among the American intellectual elite is another reason why, around the world, the phrase "American intellectual" has become an oxymoron.

In a speech on the proposed occupation of Yucatan in 1848, Calhoun said, "I have no aversion to any race, red or black, but my sympathies are for the white race."

Of course, there are whites and there are whites. A white John Kenneth Galbraith is probably higher on the ladder of whiteness than Tony Soprano. Moreover, one wonders whether Calhoun was accepted at Yale as white. His mentor, Yale President Timothy Dwight, who may have influenced Calhoun's ideas about nullification, viewed the Irish harshly. He described them as "almost absolutely uneducated, . . . bad managers, poor, and vicious."

As with most white supremacists, Calhoun's views about race and slavery are often contradictory. Calhoun blessed the contribution of mixed race people to the gene pool of South America, but ignored the growing mixed race population in South Carolina at the time. Though operations like the *New York Times*, the *New Republic,* and *Salon.com* maintain that a discussion of racial differences is a taboo, the only remaining taboo is a discussion of the mixed race heritage of most African-Americans, which resulted from sexual unions between white men and African women. Noel Ignatiev, author of *How The Irish Became White*, was right when he told an audience at Cambridge's Multicultural Arts Center that "Most blacks have some white ancestors, and many whites have some black heritage which they hide." This is the taboo discussion that both John C. Calhoun and those contemporaries who are devoted to his rhetoric ignore. Whites dominate the discussion of race in this country and their failure to address this taboo renders most discussions of race to be worthless.

The thesis of the latest book that is being praised for exposing a racial taboo, the physical superiority of black athletes, a thesis that Calhoun would endorse, is undermined by the absence of any discussion of the European heritage of most African-Americans. In his book, *Taboo: Why Black Athletes Dominate Sports and Why We Are Afraid to Talk About It*, Jon Entine treats "West Africans" and African-Americans as though their genetic history were the same. Moreover, the ancestors of those Entine refers to as "West Africans" migrated there from other parts of Africa. So mindful are Africans of the mixed genetic heritage of African-Americans (which includes Native American ancestry, documented in William Lorenz Katz's *Black Indians*), that in some parts of Africa, African-Americans are considered white.

Richard Bernstein, whose book *Dictatorship Of Virtue* ends with a rebel yell against "multiculturalism," congratulated Entine for his sophisticated argument. If Entine is sophisticated, so was John C. Calhoun, and since Gary Kamiya, an executive at *Salon.com*, praised Entine's theory (the sort that was applied to the Japanese during World War II), Calhoun is a hip post-modernist. And since *Salon* is aimed at the "upscale" yuppies, then John C. Calhoun was the great-great-granddaddy of yuppies, but instead of investing in the NASDAQ, he invested in slaves.

Calhoun also participated in the miscegenation cover-up. Writing about the differences between the races, he noted the differences distinguished by color and physical features, Entine's argument. In 1850, there were 12,000 mulatto slaves in South Carolina, many of whom were probably whiter in their features than Entine, who would be considered dark in Reykjavik, and Calhoun, whose nose shape could be found in any street corner crowd in Lagos. Calhoun must have known that many of his fellow planters had gotten it on with African women. In fact, interracial marriage was tolerated in South Carolina until 1850. As with most racial supremacists, Calhoun was incapable of spotting evidence that was right before his eyes.

His views about slavery are also inconsistent. In one speech, he congratulated whites for raising the status of the Yucatan Indians "from the condition of slaves or serfs to that of citizens and freeman," yet in other remarks, he asserted that the condition of slavery was satisfying, a positive good. In 1840, Calhoun agreed with a census report that reported a mental illness rate among free blacks as eleven times that of the slave population and used this conclusion to argue that blacks benefited from slavery. In an 1833 speech, he argued against the Force Bill, which would authorize military action to enforce the laws of Congress, particularly a tariff that worked against the South. He complained the bill would put the South in the position of a slave, requiring from it "unqualified obedience"; but in a speech delivered in 1837 he opposed those who would term slavery "immoral and sinful." With this jumping around in his opinions, Calhoun was the prototype of the neoconservative.

John McWorther, a linguist who apparently has been urged by his conservative backers to comment on subjects outside of his field, defended John Calhoun for his pro-slavery views, arguing that these views were prevalent in Calhoun's time. Not withstanding the fact that millions of blacks who lived during Calhoun's period had a different take on the slavery question from that of Calhoun, Calhoun was only pro-slavery when it came to blacks.

Calhoun's views about the positive aspects of slavery, in which generous slavemasters administered to the needs of dependent slaves, can also be found in some of America's leading intellectual journals. In a review of *Rebels on the Plantation* by John Hope Franklin, Benjamin Schwarz, who writes about black issues for *Atlantic Monthly*, the *New York Times Magazine,* and the *Los Angeles Times Book Review* from Santa Monica, California, commented about "belligerent" slaves who, by "forcing the slave community to turn to slaveholders for protection . . . compelled their fellow slaves to slip farther into dependency on whites." (Schwarz also quoted Italian-American scholar Eugene Genovese, who claimed that "Day to day resistance fostered patterns of behavior that accentuated dishonesty, trickery, and shirking," traits that are still being unfairly applied to Italian-Americans.) Booker T. Washington, however, the Tuskegee educator who was born into slavery, the son of black mother and white slaveowner, had the point of view of an eyewitness. "The slave system on our place, in large measure, took the spirit of self-reliance and self-help out of white people. My old master had many boys and girls, but not one, so far as I know, ever mastered a single trade or special line of productive industry. The girls were not taught to cook, sew, or to take care of the house. All of this was left to the slaves."

Mary Chesnut, the Martha Mitchell of the Confederacy, said that Southern white women whose husbands owned slaves were "indolent."

Whose word are we to take, that of Booker T. Washington and Mary Chesnut, who were eyewitnesses to that peculiar institution, or of Genovese and Schwarz?

Calhoun was contemporary in other ways. His obsession with states' rights is shared by many mainstream politicians today, as witnessed in the Confederate flag controversy, during which both of the leading Republican candidates, during the South Carolina primary, said that the issue ought to be left to the state. Calhoun even agrees with the Communist Manifesto—"There is and always has been in an advanced stage of wealth and civilization, a conflict between labor and capital"—and he complains about the liberal press of the time, the kind of talk one hears from right-wing callers on C-Span's *Washington Journal* each morning and on right-winger Rupert Murdoch's Fox television. Calhoun attributed the spreading of abolitionist sentiment to the abolitionists having "taken possession of the pulpit, of the schools, and, to a considerable extent, of the press; those great instruments by which the mind of the rising generation will be formed."

As for the declining morals of American society, usually fretted over by people who are hypocrites in their own lives (check out, for one, David Brock's *Blinded By The Right*), Calhoun weighed in on this issue as well and his and his wife's criticism of the morals of Andrew Jackson's administration may have cost Calhoun the presidency. The main difference between Calhoun and his contemporary followers is that Calhoun was sincere in his views about race and wasn't in it for the money. He wrote, "Of all things in the world, I have the least taste for money making, and the poorest capacity for success in it, and in particular the branch connected with stock, exchange, or banking, to which I have a peculiar aversion." He was also a man of principle. According to the historian Robert V. Remini, Calhoun, then Jackson's vice president, could have become president had he not clung so stubbornly to his theory of nullification—that the states had a right to ignore federal directives with which they disagreed, a theory that resurfaced during the civil rights movement (Andrew Jackson replied to the defiance of Calhoun and his followers by threatening them with hanging).

Those who use Calhoun's arguments against African-Americans today do so in order to raise revenue or increase the value of shares distributed by their corporations. For them it's a way of making money. I doubt whether the executives at NBC or ABC agree with Don Imus (whose slurs against blacks and gays have been documented by journalist Philip Nobile) or Rush Limbaugh, and David Talbot of *Salon* probably doesn't see eye to eye with David Horowitz, one among many American intellectuals who are wasting their talent by cashing in on the current intense resentment against African-Americans. These executives serve the masses Alpo while they dine on filet mignon.

Calhoun's tragedy was that he spent so much of his intellectual talents, which were considerable, defending an institution that held people against their will. Many of the letters between him and his friends show an obsession for inventing new arguments to justify this inhumane business.

His insistence that minority rights be protected against the tyranny of the majority has been used by members of both the left and the right, and his diehard rhetoric and resistance set the standard for some Southerners who, over 100 years after the end of the Civil War, desire to resurrect the Old South. (A secessionist party, the Southern Party, claims support from 17 percent of Southerners.) But if the *New York Times* is correct in saying that Southern values are sweeping the nation, then Calhoun has triumphed over Lincoln.

While a multibillion dollar industry has developed around the scapegoating of African-Americans, and books that "prove" their inferiority are bestsellers and are endorsed by even the "liberal" media, Lincoln's vision has faded. Speculating about what would have happened had Lincoln not been shot, giving Andrew Johnson an opportunity to return the ex-Confederate officers and politicians to power and permitting the issues that divided the states to roll over into the twentieth and twenty-first centuries, John Hope Franklin said: "We don't know, really, what [his] plans were, but I think there are some indications that he was moving toward a stand for equality, racial equality."

CHAPTER 9

The Far Right Infiltrates the Dialogue

IT'S NOT ENOUGH THAT BIG MONEY HAS CORRUPTED OUR POLITICAL system, and, through its ownership of the television networks, created a new class of legal experts and commentators who influence the outcome of court cases—replacing the traditional jury. Now, far-right money has crashed one of our most cherished institutions, the town meeting.

It was through Abigail Thernstrom's connections with the right-wing think tank the Manhattan Institute, founded by William Casey in 1978, and whose fellows include Charles Murray, co-author of *The Bell Curve*, that she was able to muscle in on the Akron, Ohio, town meeting in 1998 and thus distract from the moving testimonies about race offered by white, black, brown, and yellow citizens. It seems that the press, which often serves as a busperson for the right, would have insisted that a left-wing speaker be included in the dialogue for balance, but maybe the reason someone from a left-wing think tank wasn't included is because those think tanks don't have the kind of bucks available to them to mount the kind of campaign that got Thernstrom on.

In a July 1999 report, the National Committee for Responsive Philanthropy put at $210 million the amount that twelve foundations spent between 1992–1994 alone, "to support a wide array of conservative policy goals," among them the dismantling of affirmative action. During that period, the Manhattan Institute shelled out $2 million to fellows like Thernstrom. Another example of the institute's influence was the appearance of another of its fellows, Linda Chavez, at a December 1998 private meeting between some conservatives, who felt left out of the racial dialogue, and President Clinton and Vice President Gore.

And so without someone from the left to challenge her recycling of what even the media have regarded as myths, Thernstrom was able to turn the dialogue in Akron into a discussion of affirmative action with a president who revealed himself to be unaware of how groups other than African-Americans benefit from affirmative action.

As a result, the eloquent speeches made by the citizens of Akron were overshadowed by Abigail Thernstrom, who, because she provided the president with an antagonist, the kind of conflict that television executives crave, was given equal billing with Clinton.

Thernstrom believes that blacks would have made progress without affirmative action and that Americans are against what she calls " racial preferences." She and her husband, Stephan, wrote a book, *America in Black and White: One Nation, Indivisible.*

I wasn't surprised that David Shipler, who didn't rely on graphs, but went out and actually interviewed blacks and whites, differed with Thernstrom's rosy outlook about race relations. Historian Martin Duberman said that Shipler's book, *A Country of Strangers: Blacks and Whites in America,* "lays bare the terrifying agility of American racism." But, since Shipler's conclusions differ from those being pushed by the punditry, whose only black member seems to be the glib Armstrong Williams, most press coverage I've seen about the dialogue at Akron didn't even mention Shipler's presence.

Of course, Thernstrom has an axe to grind. Her husband got into trouble at Harvard because he offended some black women students with his remark that black men impregnate black women and then take off. He said that he was only quoting Toni Morrison. I hope that this might be a lesson to some black students about how a powerful enemy can be made by depriving someone of the opportunity to speak their minds, no matter how much we might disagree and no matter how wrong. The Thernstroms are wrong, racism hasn't become the minor problem they have painted it to be. (Recent reports, issued during the years 2001 and 2002, have cited disparities between the way blacks and whites are treated by the health industries, mortgage lending institutions, and insurance companies. Moreover racial profiling, police brutality, and harassment continue to be a problem. Though many counsel African-Americans to be patient and tolerate such insults and humiliations, very few of them would. When Gore Vidal made a remark about Abigail Thernstrom's appearance, she called him an anti-Semite without anyone accusing her of being thin-skinned or requiring her critics to behave in a P.C. manner.) African-Americans from many professions complain about harassment in everyday life.

Recently, the novelist and film writer Cecil Brown was called a "nigger" on the streets of liberal Berkeley, and when I told this to *Black Renaissance* moderator Janice Edwards, she said that she was called a "nigger bitch" on the streets of the same town. If this kind of racial enmity is happening in the capital of the counterculture, you can imagine what's happening elsewhere. Everytime I go to Georgia or Alabama, African-Americans tell me about Klan home invasions or brutality visited upon blacks, incidents that are not deemed important enough to be covered by the press.

Both President Clinton and Abigail Thernstrom erred when they supported the popular mythology that affirmative action is a black program, which, as the president said, benefits the black middle class. Hispanics, Asian-Americans, and Native Americans have also benefited from affirmative action. No matter how hard Asian-American intellectuals and journalists attempt to expose the model minority myth, the whites who dominate the dialogue on race refuse to listen. Often the racial dialogue in this country resembles the court scenes in the movie *Amistad*. Whites of opposing views arguing about the fate of African-Americans and others while the subjects of their discourse are mute or deemed unable to communicate. On January 30, 1995, a week after Ward Connerly, the black front man for anti–affirmative action forces, called for an end to affirmative action, Asian-American students from the five University of California campuses gathered in Berkeley to support the program. The students said that affirmative action was needed to remedy the "under representation of Filipino and Southeast Asian students."

Journalists and commentators who are hung up on the black-white model of race, which allows them to scapegoat black Americans for the country's social problems, have failed to notice that the Filipino-American enrollment at the University of California has also declined as a result of Proposition 209. Filipino-Americans are California's largest Asian-American group. The number of faculty women has also declined.

A report released in October 1998 by the Asian Americans/Pacific Islanders in *Philanthropy* described the model minority, an image so beloved by those who resent black Americans, as "a destructive myth." Of Asian Pacific-Americans, the report said, "As their schools fail them, these children become increasingly likely to graduate with rudimentary language skills, to drop out of school, to join gangs, or to find themselves in the low-paying occupations and on the margins of American life." So eager is the right to embarrass and humiliate blacks that the problems of millions of Asian-Americans are neglected as a result of the right's attempt to cast all Asian-Americans as valedictorians.

There was no mention at all during the town meeting at Akron of the group that benefits the most from affirmative action: white women. By deliberately casting affirmative action as a black program, its enemies are able to exploit the resentment that many white Americans harbor against black Americans for a variety of reasons. The media have found that marketing to this resentment is very profitable. When Patricia Ireland and Jesse Jackson, during a recent appearance on CNN's *Talk Back Live*, insisted that white women received the most advantages from affirmative action, the host, Susan Rook, tried to steer the conversation back to race, racial divide being a big moneymaker for CNN (which would have gone broke had it not been for the O.J. Simpson trial). Jackson termed her effort a "media violation." And so when Abigail Thernstrom repeatedly complained at Akron about racial preferences, I was wondering whether she knew that the race that seems to be preferred is the white race, if one uses primitive terms.

These white women contribute to white male prosperity. Many of them are married to white men and boost the suburban economy. Because of these women's purchasing power, I suspect that even "angry white males" are indirectly benefiting from affirmative action. Here again an intellectual from the humanities, Thernstrom, was able to get away with intellectual murder by ignoring important evidence that would undermine her arguments. Can you imagine a biologist or chemist making conclusions about a certain phenomena while ignoring one of that phenomena's most salient features the way Thernstrom and others ignore how whites benefit from affirmative action? Is it any wonder that DNA science has exploded the myth of interracial rape, which has been fostered by soft-headed thinkers, academic feminists, and sociologists, or that evidence from the mapping of the human genome has tanked the cherished opinions about "black" genes held by Jon Entine, Charles Murray, and the *New York Times* book reviewers who supported them?

Predictably, Abigail Thernstrom brought up the performance of African-Americans on SAT scores. She didn't mention, of course, that these tests have been charged with bias against women and blacks. Moreover, two investigations, by the *New York Times* and the *Wall Street Journal*, in a front-page story, have uncovered widespread suburban cheating on the tests. I've always wondered why American students sound so ignorant when polled about their knowledge about various subjects (40 percent believe that the United States fought on the side of Germany against Russia during

World War II, and one out of three students don't get science, according to the National Assessment Governing Board), yet all of a sudden get bright when taking the SATs.

Though some pundits and columnists believe that educational dumbing down only occurs in the inner city, a year 2000 report, issued by *Education Week* in collaboration with the Pew Charitable Trusts, uncovered low educational standards everywhere. Fifty-nine percent of Maine's fourth graders, for example, read below the proficiency level. (The population of Maine is 95 percent white!) Just as Asian-Americans are denied assistance because the right and even some progressives who mimic the right (it's hard to tell them apart these days) view Asian-Americans as a success story, the educational deficiencies of millions of white children are neglected, because blacks are viewed as the only educational misfits.

During the debate in Akron, Thernstrom congratulated herself on having the courage to speak frankly about race, and she repeated this praise for herself on *Hannity and Colmes*, a talk show that markets "scream" television. Thernstrom must be really insulated if she believes that people don't speak frankly about race. Don't academics read newspapers or listen to talk shows where callers and hosts outdo each other in speaking frankly about race, to their hearts content, all day? In fact those who disagree with these comments, some of which are hurtful and insulting to blacks, Hispanics, and others, are dismissed as being engaged in political correctness. Rush Limbaugh and Howard Stern, both of whom have made racially offensive remarks, have millions of followers. People like Andy Rooney and Professor Lino Graglia, who said that Mexican-, African-, and Sicilian-Americans were against achievement, are made into national heroes for their insulting remarks about minorities. Every morning on radio and MSNBC, Imus and his colleagues have a good-old-boy time mimicking the black English of black athletes and other personalities. If Thernstrom had tuned into the comments by callers to C-Span immediately following the Akron dialogue, she would have heard people speaking frankly about race, some of it mean-spirited and racist.

Having played the race card and the model minority card, toward the end of the dialogue, Thernstrom started to play the immigrant card, about how immigrants have succeeded where blacks haven't. I'm sure that she would have ignored millions of immigrants who are mired in poverty, some of whom are subjected to a worse tangle of pathologies than those that the press attributes to the inner cities exclusively.

I thought that the dialogue in Akron was a good start, but I would hope that in the future, black, brown, white, and yellow citizens will be able to debate the issue of race head-on without well-funded interlopers, performance intellectuals, and academics out to hawk their books butting in.

The most important point made during the town meeting was made by a businessman who said that diversity is good for business. Whether diversity, affirmative action, or mutliculturalism survive will not depend upon the go-fors on behalf of right-wing think tanks, or turncoat progressives, but by business.

Even the businesses that fund the right-wing spokespersons seem divided about these matters. While some of the people from the Heritage Foundation oppose gay marriage and "identity politics," Coors, one of the foundation's sponsors, is courting black and gay sales. One of the foundation's founders has been identified by David Brock as having "a history of associating with anti-Semites and racists." The ironies and contradictions of the right continue.

CHAPTER 10

The "C" Word

SIX YEARS AGO, ROBERT S. BOYNTON IN THE *ATLANTIC MONTHLY* nominated a group of new black intellectuals whom he hailed for going beyond race to look at the "commonality of American concern." Yet if race were placed in the background of their work, none of the writers and thinkers he mentioned would be in business.

Americans are fascinated with race, and so it is inevitable that merely placing the word "nigger" on the cover of a book guarantees controversy and book sales. And because *Nigger* is a book written by an African-American, a professor at Harvard Law School at that, the book title is a strategy that creates a rift among the African-American intelligentsia, many of whom seem to be proxies for white, neoliberal opinion. As Lewis Lapham, editor of *Harper's*, said of one of the chosen, "He says what we say in private."

No wonder these writers receive such an uncritical free pass in those publications whose opinions they mirror. Sometimes it appears that these black intellectuals are willing to sacrifice scholarship for the sake of publicity and cash. When Henry Louis Gates Jr., who has described himself as an "intellectual entrepreneur," was assembling a staff to compile an encyclopedia of black history, only three of the forty full-time writers and editors brought to the project, *Encarta Africana*, were black. In addition, according to *Mother Jones* magazine, Gates and his co-editor, K. Anthony Appiah, turned down requests from white staffers to hire more African-Americans.

Works of dubious scholarly merit are given inflated advances by publishers. Nearly nine years ago, for example, Michael Lerner and Cornel West were awarded a reported $100,000 advance for their slim collection of essays, *Jews & Blacks: A Dialogue on Race, Religion, and Culture in America*. Some of these works are rewritings of other works and contain no new or original insights. John McWorther (*Losing the Race*) writes about black "victimization," a territory already exhausted by Shelby Steele, a much better and more thoughtful writer. McWorther goes so far as to say that blacks are "anti-intellectual" when, according to Martin Arnold of the *New York Times*, since September 11, 2001, blacks are buying books in numbers that seem to be "a bit better than [in] white mainstream publishing."

The goal of the black intelligentsia, it might be argued, is to justify white opinion that might seem racist. For example, Orlando Patterson, another member of the Talented Tenth—W. E. B. DuBois's name for the black intellectual vanguard—says that whites moved to the suburbs because of the bad behavior of black school students, which doesn't explain why whites segregate themselves from model minorities like Cuban-Americans. Randall Kennedy himself has played to irrational white fears by arguing that whites have a right to avoid young blacks because of crime statistics, yet, more than 75 percent of violent crimes against whites are committed by other whites. Given this fact, why aren't white women afraid to board elevators with white men? In an unscholarly fashion, the Talented Tenth often ignore facts that might challenge their premises. For example, Gates, in his standard "tough love" speech, scolds "thirty-five-year-old black grandmothers living in the projects"; what he and his friends fail to mention is that the "out-of-wedlock" birthrate among black women has plummeted faster than that of any other ethnic group. It took conservative columnist Ben Wattenberg to comment about this trend.

Kennedy's book, *Nigger*, is being sold on the basis of the questions it answers. "How should 'nigger' be defined?" Kennedy asks. "Is it part of the American cultural inheritance that warrants preservation? . . . Should blacks be able to use 'nigger' in ways forbidden to others? Should the law view 'nigger' as a provocation strong enough to reduce the culpability of a person who responds violently to it? Under what circumstances, if any, should a person be ousted from his or her job for saying 'nigger'? What methods are useful for depriving 'nigger' of destructiveness?"

In other words, Kennedy's new book provides guidelines about when it's appropriate to use the word and when it's not. Under some conditions, he argues, whites should be able to use the word regardless of "the embarrassment and hurt feelings the term inflicts." The short book, an expanded essay, includes four sections, of which two, "The Protean N-Word" and the "Pitfalls in Fighting 'Nigger,'" are sometimes interesting. All four sections include anecdotes, folklore, and memoirs of celebrities about the use of the word "nigger." Its history is explored and the use of the word by famous comedians such as Richard Pryor are cited. Pryor stopped using the word after a trip to Africa. We learn that Lenny Bruce used the word to weaken its potency, to "defang" the word, a strategy of which Kennedy approves. He also analyzes the motives of whites and blacks for using the word.

Most of the analysis is light. For blacks, Kennedy argues, the term can be a positive, but it can also reflect self-hatred. If Kennedy believes that self-hatred is unique to African-Americans, he knows very little about America's other ethnic groups. Attributing certain attitudes exclusively to blacks is a common practice of the black intelligentsia, for whom African-Americans are the most homophobic, misogynistic, or anti-Semitic of all ethnic groups. This approach exposes the one-dimensionality of their thought. They just haven't studied other American ethnic groups.

Kennedy also accuses blacks of being oversensitive about the use of the word "nigger." If they're oversensitive, they're not the only ethnic group to be offended by ethnic slurs. In fact, based upon my reading, I would say that blacks are the least thin-skinned of American ethnic groups. They are constantly ridiculed in Hollywood movies and on television. Booker T. Washington complained about the press coverage of blacks almost 100 years ago. To expose the warts of others—even in ridicule—is considered by some to reveal the secrets of the community or to provide the enemy with ammunition, but it is done to the African-American community with relative impunity.

I found reading through the section "'Nigger' in Court" to be rough sledding. Kennedy discusses cases in which jurors, lawyers, or jurists have referred to blacks as "niggers." (Whites who deny that racism exists in the criminal justice system will be shocked by this, just as they were shocked by the revelation that some Los Angeles policemen plant evidence.) In addition, he examines cases in which a black person used the "fighting-word" defense when charged with assaulting a white person who used the word, cases in which racial slurs are used on the job or in commerce, and, finally, cases in which witnesses or litigants use the term. Kennedy contends that a white person's calling a black person "nigger" is no excuse for harming that person and that blacks should show Ellisonian patience when assaulted by the term. When I read this line, all I could think of was what Julian Bond once wrote:

"Look at that girl shake that thing/We all can't be Martin Luther King."

Kennedy believes that if a black person and a white person are intimates, then it's all right for the white person to call his friend a "nigger": "Can a relationship between a black person and a white one be such that the white person should properly feel authorized, within the confines of that relationship, to use the N-word? For me the answer is yes."

He also approves of Harry Truman's and Lyndon Johnson's use of the word because they inaugurated programs that were beneficial to black people. (He could have included Abraham Lincoln who, according to historian Lerone Bennett Jr., used "nigger" often and loved minstrel shows so much that sometimes he would miss appointments to attend one.)

Kennedy's comments about the use of the word by rappers show the isolation of the Talented Tenth. They live in academic settings, white enclaves, such as Cambridge, Massachusetts, and New Haven, Connecticut, and don't have a clue about Compton. Ice-T, in a recent interview, said that some of the rappers were former criminals who condoned the drugging of African-Americans from 1984 until recently, so long as they could make a profit from it. He said that with Hip Hop, they became legitimate. In his film *Images of Hip-Hop in the Bay Area,* author Cecil Brown interviews some rappers. They come across as cynical, amoral capitalists who know what turns on their white suburban audience. This audience seems to need its "nigger" fix. Rather than being heroes who use the word as a sign of independence, as Kennedy would have us believe, these rappers are merely marketing a product. "These entertainers don't care whether whites are confused by blacks' use of the term," he writes. "And they don't care whether whites who hear blacks using the N-word think that African Americans lack self-respect. The black comedians and rappers who use and enjoy 'nigger' care principally, perhaps exclusively, about what they themselves think, desire and enjoy—which is part of their allure."

A few years ago novelist Charles Johnson and I were sitting in the rear of a room where white professors were arguing about whether Mark Twain had a right to use the word. They used the word with what I felt to be excessive enthusiasm, as though they were high on something, as though the word were some form of verbal crack. Johnson turned to me and said, "What am I doing here?" Many black readers will probably feel the same way when reading Kennedy's book.

—An earlier version of this essay
appeared in *Los Angeles Times,*
February 3, 2002

CHAPTER 11

The Rest of Us Are Arab

MY MOTHER NAMED ME AFTER HER FAVORITE COUSIN, AND A few weeks ago at the St. Louis airport, the salesperson asked me whether I was a Muslim. I said no, but when I arrived at the baggage claims section at the San Francisco airport, I noticed that mine was the only luggage with a red tag attached to it. Maybe the red tag meant "this is a wonderful person," but how would I know? It was an unsettling experience.

Within two weeks after the WTC and Pentagon bombings, my youngest daughter, Tennessee, was called a dirty Arab, twice. An elderly white woman made such a scene on a San Francisco bus that my daughter got off. That time, she was wearing a scarf that I bought her in Egypt last year, but on the other occasion there was nothing distinctive about her clothing. Some of the post–9-11 profiling would be comic and ironic if the circumstances weren't so tragic. Marvin X, an African-American playwright, has been criticizing some Arab-American owners of ghetto stores for selling pork, alcohol, and drugs and extending credit to poor women in exchange for sexual favors. A few days after the terrorist attack, he was surrounded by men with guns at Newark airport. They mistook him for an Arab terrorist.

The experience of me, my daughter, and Marvin X points to the problem with flashing a searchlight upon an entire community, which is what's being done to Arab-Americans by many white Americans, who've become apprehensive as they move about their daily lives.

But who's Arab? A few years ago, journalist Earl Caldwell and I entertained over thirty Arab journalists at the Maynard Institute in Oakland. Their escort, an Arab-American attorney, said that he'd been stopped, while driving an expensive car, because the police mistook him for a black American. Is anyone with a dark skin Arab-American? Should those who are caught in the net meant for Arab-Americans follow the example of some Chinese-Americans who, when the Japanese-Americans were herded into detention camps, wore signs that read "I Am Chinese"?

The Bush administration has taken advantage of the hysteria that's been ignited by the media and other institutions to jam a "Patriot" bill through Congress. This bill gives the executive branch tremendous powers with very little judicial review. The government detained over a thousand people, some of them incommunicado, and refused to identify who is being detained and why when requested to do so by Senator Russ Feingold. The administration wants to monitor communications between lawyers and their clients. The Justice Department is questioning 5,000 Muslim men, a procedure that Feingold describes as "offensive" and "intrusive." They established military tribunals without consulting the Defense Department or Congress. (Military tribunals that are opposed by the Spanish government!)

Given President Bush's switch-happy record as Texas executioner, I'd hate to be one of those tried. Senator Edward Kennedy has criticized such tribunals for their lack of "openness" and "fairness" and "due process." Burma, Nigeria, Turkey, and Egypt are among the countries where such military tribunals are used. Now the United States.

Some have complained that the United States is becoming a "banana republic" as a result of the 9-11 events. William Safire, a *New York Times* columnist and a genuine conservative (not just one who plays the role on TV), calls these powers "dictatorial."

Arab-Americans won't be the first group to be singled out for scorn as a result of international events over which they have no control. Professor Lois Fassbinder writes about the prejudice her German-American family experienced during World War II. During the same war, hundreds of Italian immigrants were interned and thousands had their travel restricted by the Justice Department. Italian-Americans were forced from their homes and required to submit to hearings before military tribunals. Some members of both groups were able to deal with such humiliation by turning "white"— an option that is open to those with white skins and maybe open to white-skinned Arab-Americans. (As Malcolm X discovered during his trip to the Middle East, Islam includes members of all races.) They can change their names and disappear into the white world.

But this has its drawbacks, too. A few years ago, I was a panelist at an Irish-American writers conference. At the end of the panel, I asked members of the audience if assimilation had been worth it. None of the audience members said yes. Some complained that they had to change their names and marry Anglos in order to get jobs. They had to give up their roots.

Decades after World War II, the United States apologized to the Japanese-American community for the internment but, judging from the complaints of some contemporary Japanese-American poets and novelists who were children in those camps, the psychic scars remain.

With the exception of Native Americans, however, no group has been terrorized as much as African-Americans by the kind of home-grown terrorists about whom the Justice Department seems indifferent. Maybe the experience of African-Americans will be a guide to all Americans about how to handle both profiling and terrorism.

Martin Luther King Jr. was an object of hate crimes and his home was bombed. He didn't go into a funk and yield to his tormentors, but persisted. Both Booker T. Washington and Frederick Douglass were born slaves; their lives were at risk every day. In their lectures, they always warned their white audiences that if such outrages could happen to blacks they could happen to them as well. Now the president and the attorney general are hunting Arab-Americans. Who's next?

**—An earlier version of this essay appeared
on Time.com on December 6, 2001**

CHAPTER 12

The New Teutonics

BRILL'S CONTENT MAGAZINE, WHICH OFTEN SERVES AS A monitor for media excess, has identified, in its March 2001 edition, a trend in television news, as the networks compete with one another for ratings—an emphasis on what divides us. During the stalemate over the presidential vote count in Florida, the network's marketing angle became "a nation divided." A "nation divided" soon became a product that has become commercially profitable over the last few years, "a racial divide." White Americans became Wyatt Earp and Doc Holliday gunning for Black America, the bad guys hankering for a showdown at a racial OK Corral. The media sold the tickets to whites who had resentments against blacks as diverse as Clarence Thomas and Maxine Waters. Clarence Thomas had it right at least once when he said that he was subjected to a high-tech lynching. Indeed, the Thomas/Anita Hill hearings might be considered by later media historians as the beginning of the time when reality unscripted television replaced the soap operas as the focus for national obsessions.

Next came the O. J. Simpson case, in which, for television, Simpson was the last survivor on the island, Nicole Simpson and Ron Goldman having been killed off. Following this spectacle were the Clinton scandals and impeachment, which lifted television vérité to an international level.

When I visited Nigeria, in 1999, I found intellectuals tuned into every episode. It is not surprising that these media carnivals would feature two black actors and a white Negro. If one reads the history of slavery and its aftermath, Reconstruction and the redemption of the South, which came about as the result of terrorism, one can discover the traditional role of blacks in the United States. Not only were blacks a cheap labor supply, but they were used as models for advertising and sources for entertainment. Some whites have made millions by imitating blacks, from the days of the minstrels to Eminem, Don Imus, and the Al Jolson imitator David Horowitz. Imus and his cohorts entertain the Anglos in Kennebunkport and other rich Ports by blackening up each morning and showing their mastery of their version of Ebonics:

Imus: Here now, Bernard McGuirk as Maya Angelou.

McGuirk: How you doin'? (Extended laughter) The Yankees freed you from chains/They gave the South a lickin'/Not so you could smoke crack, get bitches and eat lots of chicken. (Extended laughter)

Imus (seeming amused): No, no, no, no, no, Maya.

McGuirk: Show some pride/Stop you're whinin' and sayin' o po me/And shaking you booty to me so hor-ny.

Imus (faking exasperation): That'll be fine, Maya.

McGuirk: Got a cigarette? (Laughter)

Eminem is Jewish and Imus is Celtic, groups that were despised in a former time by self-styled Teutonics and who are still the victims of slights and hate crimes. Those whom we refer to as Rednecks are probably Celtic-American. While the media lash out at smalltime African-American anti-Semites, the real anti-Semites, the ones with the power to influence public policy, are pushing for a Christian nation. While Eminem delights the suburbs and the white critics who've been longing for a white hope who would dominate Hip Hop sales, Don Imus delights the cognoscenti in a manner that would have been considered racist in a former time, but is now considered a courageous stance against political correctness in this period of the Second Confederate Redemption, in which individuals with generous access to the media slam African-Americans who have little. Remember the Michigan student who referred to black coeds as Water Buffaloes? What the good old boys, who embraced racist comments of Andy Rooney, Jimmy Breslin, and Daniel Moynihan, left out, when praising him, was that he also told these women to go to the zoo. Telling black women to go to the zoo is a no-no, in a country where black women have been regarded as beasts. Booker T. Washington, the great educator, said that his white father, a slave owner, gave his mother the same regard that one would give a cow.

When I learned, during an appearance of the Imus group on C-Span, that these performers were Irish and Scots-Irish, it all made sense. I wonder if these new Teutonics, those who are passing for white, were aware that the old Teutonics, stateside white supremacists who claimed to have pure white blood, had a saying: "The solution of the American race problem is to have an Irishman kill a black man and get hanged for it." In those days things weren't so black and white. Don Imus and his friends wouldn't have found it so easy to pass for white. But casting things as black and white may be an easy way to get ratings to climb and provide ex-ethnics with a whiteness upgrade, but it doesn't define an America that is no longer blackening up and whitening up, but coloring up. But the opinionmakers haven't be dissuaded from their obsession with a black-and-white America.

The racial divide holds that blacks and whites form separate cultural and epistemological nations. On one side are the whites who are devoted to family, hard work, and reason. On the other side are blacks who are lazy, dysfunctional, and irrational. Blacks think in terms of urban myths. Spokespersons for the white side maintain that racism is dead and that when blacks complain about racism, they're playing the race card. Never mind the mountain of data that have proven that blacks, Hispanics, and Asian-Americans are still discriminated against. Some white commentators argue that racism is not dead, because African-Americans are racists. This is a switch from the conclusions of the 1960s Kerner Report, which blamed whites for racism. When the *New York Times* did a series on blacks recently, written by a team of reporters, most of whom were white, it was the blacks who were the racists.

Much sympathy was given to a white man who came under criticism for using the word "niggardly." The view that whites are the real victims of racism is nothing new. George Washington said that it was his "misfortune" to own slaves, never mind how his slaves felt. Coverage of black issues by the New York Times epitomizes the new thinking on race. When its reporters and editors cover issues about race, they have already made up their minds about issues affecting black Americans and merely go out to find some anecdotes to back them up. A conservative, James Traub, in an article praising Mayor Rudolph Giuliani, actually found some inner-city residents who said that they didn't mind being stopped and frisked. Recently, a group of young people found the New York Times's coverage of black and white teens to be different. The young black and Hispanic teens charged with crimes are usually shown shackled, while yearbook photos identified the white teen offenders. When the youth approached the Times about the result of their study they were given the brush-off.*

This is another example of the media dividing Americans, serving as a cheerleader for the white side and protecting them from images that might embarrass them. In 2001, a New York Times reporter went to Harlem and only found crack and dysfunctionality, while a story about skyrocketing heroin abuse in the suburbs only received a few lines. Some of those who deliver Las Vegas decisions to the black side of the media-engendered racial divide are, like Don Imus, once regarded as members of a separate race, before they were awarded whiteness. Some of them, like Imus, were Irish or Scots-Irish; others were Eastern European Jews whom, ironically, upstanding citizens were advised to avoid.

The descendants of the once politically radical Lower East Siders now fill the ranks of the American Enterprise Institute, which

---

*The Study was conducted by We INTERRUPT This Message, a national media training and strategy center, and Youth Force, a youth-led South Bronx organizing group.

two black conservatives found so racist that they resigned. When I tune into cable television to watch these third- and fourth-generation types screaming their lungs out, baiting black leaders and criticizing blacks for every conceivable offense, I wonder whether they know that the same vicious invective was once aimed at their groups.

Some of them are hypocrites who demand of blacks standards to which they can't abide. I identified some in a *Baltimore Sun* article. The late labor writer for a Chicago paper who criticized blacks for their violence took a swing at a policeman when arrested for DUI. A neoconservative who argued that blacks should abide by bourgeoisie values was outed by *Vanity Fair* as a cocaine addict, and Andrew Sullivan, whose defense of *The Bell Curve* while editor of the *New Republic* brought him to the attention of the *New York Times Magazine*, from which he launched tough-love lectures against blacks and gays. (He was recently exposed as a practitioner of "bareback," or unprotected, sex.) As for two of the most recent presidents, both of whom campaigned by preaching tough love to black people, attending churches and recovery centers, urging blacks to improve their moral behavior and act responsibly, one was almost impeached for covering up an affair, and the other was revealed on the eve of the election to have a DUI arrest. We have a president and vice president who have three DUIs between them.

And what of the millions who don't fit in the racial divide? The acquittal of O. J. Simpson in the criminal trial was supposed to have reflected a racial divide. Yet, at the time, before the media insisted upon a different verdict, *USA Today* did a poll which found that whites were split about the verdict. Where do the 44 percent who agreed with the decision in the criminal case belong? Did they defect to the black side of the racial divide? Are they race traitors?

Even Salon.com, which is supposed to be hip, bought into racial-divide journalism. Salon.com said that the reaction of blacks in Florida to the Scalia coup was an example of the racial divide. Yet millions of whites also believe that the election was stolen. Have they gone over to the enemy's side? And what about Mexican-Americans, Puerto Ricans, and Cuban-Americans? And what about

Asian-Americans, a catch-all term for many ethnic groups? Where are they in the media's racial divide? Are the Hispanics and Asian-Americans an extracontinental invasion force, awaiting the results of the struggle between black and white America before deciding which side to join?

Even though the census indicates that Hispanics and blacks have equal numbers in the United States population, Hispanics are rarely included in the racial debate. (And, no sooner had these numbers been released than a reporter for NPR, which can do the racial-divide thing as well as the corporate media, asked his Hispanic and black guests whether this meant that there will be tensions between blacks and Hispanics.)

When NBC released a poll about police brutality in New York, the fact that Hispanics agreed with African-Americans that brutality was a problem was ignored. Are all blacks and whites loyal soldiers to the two sides of the racial divide? Based upon my travels through different cultural and ethnic villages, I would doubt whether things are as simple as a media, which make their money from conflict and simplifying, would have us believe. Let me give you an example of my interaction with the groups that make up the American mosaic.

In 1998, I published a book entitled *Multi-America: Essays on Cultural War and Cultural Peace*, which included the viewpoints of writers from different backgrounds about some of the persistent issues of American life. This book was celebrated by the Italian-American Society at a Barnes and Noble bookstore in New York. On September 26, 1998, I was inducted into the Tlingit tribe during ceremonies at Sitka, Alaska, during an all day potlatch ceremony. In the same year, I was the guest of Asian-American students at the University of California at Davis. In February 1999, I traveled to Nigeria, which is undergoing the kind of ethnic wars that characterized the United States in the nineteenth century, when the Scots-Irish and the Anglo tribes fought each other in what we call the Civil War, and the Irish, blacks, and other ethnics were used to subdue Native American ethnics.

I recently published 25 New Nigerian Poets as a result of my visit. It is the literary event of the year, in Nigeria. In April 1999, I appeared before the Irish Historical and Literary Society. It was here that I presented a talk entitled "The Self-Loathing Ethnic As an Obstacle to Racial Harmony." Among other points I made was that those ex-ethnics who have made a profession of slamming African-Americans do so not only for a generous paycheck, but because African-Americans remind them of the ethnicities they have fled.

While visiting Israel a few months ago, I complained about Saul Bellow and Philip Roth, two Jewish-American novelists, who blast African-Americans in book after book. An Israeli writer reminded me that these two have problems with Jewish women, too. I told the audience that the "Anglo-Saxon cultural occupation has required all groups, whether Latinos, Asian-Americans, Afro-Americans, or European-Americans, to discard their heritages to become part of the mainstream culture, and that to make it in America, many Irishmen and women dropped their brogue, changed their names to Anglo names and married into Anglo families." I reminded the audience that James T. Farrell, the Irish-American author, said that when the Irish left Chicago for the suburbs, they left Ireland.

While many European-Americans have abandoned their European origins and many Asian-Americans have abandoned Asia, most African-Americans never completely abandoned Africa, and whenever I visit Africa, I'm struck by how much African-Americans have maintained their African style and how much they have lost. (One loss is the lack of reverence for the elderly and for nature on the part of some. If African-American children were aware of their traditions, they wouldn't throw stones at animals, or take down my lemons before they were ripe. Some African children can identify over 500 plants.) So what annoys the new Teutonics about African-Americans is that they are still "old country" in some sense. The new Teutonics congratulate other groups for imitating their assimilationist strategies. Their refusal to include facts that would undercut their opinions of blacks renders their observations propaganda.

The syndicated columnist Mona Charen, who makes a living criticizing blacks in the same manner that whites have been criticizing her people for centuries, wonders why American blacks can't be like African immigrants. She doesn't tell you that among immigrants, Africans have the highest scholastic attainment.

Some tough-love critics of blacks want to know why African-Americans can't emulate the successes of Korean mom-and-pop store owners in New York. What they don't tell you is that 70 percent of these store owners have college degrees.

Why can't you be like Asian-Americans, the critics ask? They don't tell you about the poverty among Southeast Asian-Americans or the discrimination against Filipino-Americans, whom some Asian-Americans refer to with the N word. You don't see Asian-Americans asking for affirmative action, they claim. They don't tell you when Proposition 209 was being discussed, Asian-American groups met at the University of California at Berkeley and said that they needed it.

Does affirmative action lower standards, which is the argument of the most recent black hustler making money by cashing in on white resentment of blacks? Well, Helen Zia said that she benefited from affirmative action, and I don't see how anyone can read her excellent book, *Asian American Dreams*, and say that she has lowered standards. When Niger Innis got up on MSNBC, which makes money from dissing blacks, and said that affirmative action harmed Asian-Americans, I yelled at the set, "You don't know what you're talking about."

Why don't you be like Jewish-Americans? The tough-love critics don't tell you about the hundreds of thousands of Jews who haven't made it, or the Hasidic families living in Crown Heights on food stamps. Everybody can't be like the Jewish hired hands of Rupert Murdoch who scold blacks in his many publications, the Jews whom I referred to as the Ersatz. They who abandoned their Jewishness and joined in on the vilification of African-Americans.

Though those blacks who have uttered anti-Semitic remarks

have been denounced in the press and have even been condemned by Congress, those Jews who stereotype African-Americans do so with little fear of the fierce repudiation the media have aimed at black anti-Semites. In fact, a sensational press has even infected public opinion with the poison that the last vestiges of anti-Semitism exists among the black population. When I visited Israel in December 2000, I found that even among writers and intellectuals the opinion existed that every African-American is an anti-Semite. I took my concerns about this inflated black-Jewish feud to *Tikkun* magazine, edited by Rabbi Michael Lerner, which was published there. If there was resentment against some Jews it was mostly among black intellectuals and some professionals. This was a resentment based on the feeling that some Jews had gone "white" on them. In my opinion, Herbert Hill, former labor secretary for the N.A.A.C.P., wrote the best essay about the media-hyped Jewish-black feud. Hill said that the Jews became white in the 1960s. Before that, a right-wing Jew was considered an oxymoron. In her book *How the Jews Became White Folks*, author Karen Brodkin makes the same point.

Noel Ignatiev, author of *How the Irish Became White*, said it all:

> Whiteness is not a culture. There is an Irish culture and Italian culture and American culture—the latter, as Albert Murray pointed out, a mixture of Yankee, the Indian, and the Negro (with a pinch of ethnic salt); there is youth culture and drug culture and queer culture; but there is no such thing as white culture. Whiteness . . . is nothing but a reflection of privilege, and exists for no reason other than to defend it.

—An earlier version of this essay was delivered before the Irish Studies Colloquium, University of California at Davis, March 9, 2001

CHAPTER 13

Teaching Poetry to the *Star Trek* Generation

WHAT KIND OF COUNTRY WOULD THE UNITED STATES BE IF every person transformed a personal grudge against an individual into a vendetta against a whole class of people? A woman has an unhappy experience with a man and as a result takes it out on all men. Or a man is injured by a woman and becomes a misogynist as a result. What would the nature of social relations be if blacks held a grudge against all whites for the daily insults they receive from a few anonymous whites? And what if they were media moguls or paid-for public intellectuals who were able to shape opinion and policy by casting all whites in a disparaging light based upon their interaction with a few? And suppose that these people had unlimited access to air their views and monopolized free speech so that those without resources had little ability to counter their views. How would white people in this country feel?

Reading the background of some of those former liberals who moved to neoconservatism, I'm struck by how many trace their ideological shift to an encounter with a black person or a group of black men. Irving Kristol said that a neoconservative is a liberal who has been mugged by reality.

Since the typical mugger is depicted as a black man, I took that

to mean that neoconservatives are those liberals who had unfortu-
nate encounters with black men. David Kennedy, who views crime
in more depth than bumper-sticker thinking, and who has been
part of a team that has reduced the Boston crime rate, said that
crimes are committed by about 1,200 people in that town, those
who are repeated felons who've been arrested about ten times.
They are under 1 percent of the population. Most people who get
their information from television probably don't realize that 94 percent of African-American youth are not involved in the criminal
justice system. And so, based on the actions of a few, Irving Kristol
was indicting a whole class, a technique that's been used against
the Jews for hundreds of years.

David Horowitz, who has been able to raise millions of dollars to
carry on a well-publicized feud with black people, said that he shifted
to neoconservatism because the Black Panthers murdered a friend of
his. Joan Walsh, who describes herself as a "white woman scorned,"
as a result of a failed relationship with a black man, is Horowitz's en-
abler at *Salon.com*. She said that David Horowitz has "convincing" evidence that the Panthers are guilty of the murder, yet neither
Horowitz nor Walsh has turned this evidence over to the police.

Walsh has vented her anger against her former lover with a series of articles designed to hurt blacks or stir up resentment against
blacks. To show how blind rage can be, she, like some of the others
who feel wounded by a black or a group of blacks, doesn't always
adhere to the facts. I corrected her when she said that black people
have gained advantages at the expense of others. I reminded her
that most of those who have benefited from social programs have
been whites. The beneficiaries of affirmative action have been
white women, yet John McWorther appeared on National Public
Radio in a program that described affirmative action as a "racial
preference" program. If there's a racial preference to affirmative action, then it's for the white race. During this program, McWorther
was allowed to run amuck with his usual tall tales and anecdotes
about blacks lowering standards by accepting affirmative action,

but not once suggesting that white women have lowered standards. If he'd done that, the feminists who run NPR wouldn't have invited McWorther to appear. McWorther said that when he was a kid, he was teased by other black kids because he was such a nerd.

One reads this kind of statement about blacks regularly in the press. I guess that these op-ed writers and journalists have been done wrong by black lovers or were teased by blacks or beaten up by blacks.

Another couple who have black people on the brain are Stephan and Abigail Thernstrom. I'm sure that Philip Roth used Thernstrom's problems at Harvard as the model for the character in his book *The Human Stain*. In this book it is proposed that if you say boo to black students you'll have problems. If Roth believes this, he's another American writer who is alienated from the experiences of black people. In this book he is a defender of high culture, which he views as being under assault by the black hordes. Before blacks arrived in Newark, New Jersey, in large numbers, Roth suggested, in novel after novel, that the city was some kind of fifth-century Athens. By the way, my definition of an American advocate of high culture is someone who can't read Euripides in the Greek.

Another man who is sore about black people is Marty Peretz of the *New Republic*. He was once a member of Students for a Democratic Society, wouldn't you know, and traces his problems with black people to some blacks equating Zionism with racism. Since then Peretz has used his magazine, the *New Republic*, to showcase his problems with black people. He got into trouble from some quarters when he said that blacks suffered from a cultural deficiency, but he drew defense from others. For Accuracy in Reporting, an organization devoted to monitoring right-wing bias in the media, asked some of those who had condemned the Rev. Louis Farrakhan's referring to Judaism as "a gutter religion" whether they would condemn Peretz for his remarks about black women. Farrakhan's ideas were proclaimed as "unhealthy" in a hit piece written by Henry Louis Gates Jr. for the *New Yorker* when it was edited by Tina Brown. But when Brown was asked by F.A.I.R. to repudiate

Peretz's remarks about black women, she said that she'd have to study them before replying. After this incident, it must have occurred to Peretz that the solution to this problem, that of seeming backward and bigoted, was to hire someone who resembled the group that had caused him so much anxiety. Enter John Mc-Worther. Hiring someone from a minority group to front bigoted opinions is a game with endless variations. After having come under attack from African-Americans for its portrayal of African-Americans, the *New York Times Magazine* hired Andrew Sullivan to hound African-Americans about political correctness, that stuck record from which the right won't remove the needle. Sullivan must have come to the attention of the *New York Times's* editors after an incident at the *New Republic* when he caused an uproar by defending Charles Murray's notorious *The Bell Curve*. For someone who is interested in IQ tests, it seems contradictory that Sullivan endorsed George Bush for president. Moreover, one of Sullivan's targets has been affirmative action, yet Gore Vidal said that Sullivan wouldn't have achieved prominence had he not been gay.

I also had an interesting exchange with Richard Lowry, editor of the *National Review*. He said that, in the case of George Bush, IQ didn't matter, it was judgment that counted. I sent an e-mail asking why the *National Review*, an Irish-American publication, endorsed *The Bell Curve* and George Bush. He said that the book didn't cover politicians. His weak response was, "I don't think Charles Murray said anything about connection between IQ and political leadership. But correct me if I'm wrong."

John McWorther is a professor of linguistics at the University of California at Berkeley. He is the author of a book of throwaway lines called *Losing the Race: Self-Sabotage in Black America*. He became upset with me because I said that I'd read his book in thirty minutes and referred to it as breezy. He threatened to "wipe up the floor with me in debate"; however, after my comments dogged him from publication to publication he stipulated to a journalist that he'd only submit to an interview if Ishmael Reed and that gang weren't quoted.

(When I finally accepted McWorther's challenge to a debate, he backed down.) I found McWorther easy reading because his theories or whatever you want to call them about black self-victimization and self-sabotage have already been pronounced much more eloquently by Shelby Steele and more colorfully by Stanley Crouch. Discovering why some people are fascinated or obsessed with this subject so that they never seem to get enough of it may recommend a new field of psychiatry. Mona Charen, another person who supports her suburban lifestyle by ragging African-Americans, quoted me in the *Washington Times* as referring to McWorther as a "rent-a-black."

Maybe that was rude, but not as rude as his reference to a campus group to which my daughter belongs. After the group BAMN, By Any Means Necessary, challenged McWorther to a debate about his views on affirmative action, he refused. He called them "stupid idiots" and a "real fart of an organization." I should have referred to McWorther in more civil manner. Maybe I should have called him a proxy black, someone who fronts the opinions of others. And so it wasn't surprising that McWorther appeared in Marty Peretz's *New Republic*. In a review of Donald Bogle's *Primetime Blues: African-Americans On Network Television*, McWorther became—you've heard of the body double who is used to substitute for that of a star—Peretz's mind double, accusing black people of self-sabotage, the kind of opinion product that gets him airtime on places like Fox and MSNBC, outfits that view black thrashing as a way of boosting their audience. McWorther opposed the idea that blacks are stereotyped in television roles, a fact that's been documented by a number of studies, including two from the Civil Rights Commission (and in May 2002 by a Children Now study, which can be found at ChildrenNow.org), and said that there were empirical studies to support his opinion. Typical of the fast and loose opinionizing of public intellectuals, McWorther didn't cite any. The gist of his book, according to Charen, is that blacks are anti-intellectual. George Will, who uses his *Newsweek* column to deliver sanctimonious lectures to blacks about morality, when his own morals have been brought into question, also praised McWorther's idea about anti-intellectualism. The article was entitled "The Ultimate Emancipation." For Will, who once said that in comparison to blacks, whites were an advanced race, the ultimate emancipation for blacks would occur when "blacks reject victimology and separatism as a coping strategy and anti-intellectualism." Will's blanket characterization of the attitudes of black people demonstrates that just having a black editor at the helm of a mass magazine doesn't mean that generalizing about the behavior of black people will cease.

McWhorter and others, whom he mimics, usually point to the performance of blacks on SAT scores, without including the criticism of such tests by Fair Tests and other organizations. Nor is it mentioned by McWhorter's supporters the hundreds of millions of dollars that African-Americans are spending on books, the proliferation of websites devoted to black literature, the appearance of black authors on the bestsellers' lists. During the controversy about McWhorter's refried opinions, few noticed that Terry McMillan's *A Day Late And A Dollar Short*, an outstanding literary achievement, made it to the top of the *New York Times's* bestsellers list.

The reading scores of black students have also drawn the criticism of those who accuse African-Americans of "self-sabotage." These test scores do look pretty bad until you compare them with those of the others. Lost in the Ebonics controversy of a few years ago was the fact that Hispanic students do worse than blacks. Even the *New York Times*, which ties the poverty of African-Americans to their moral failings, had to admit that the highest dropout rate occurs among Hispanic girls (but chose the photos of black Hispanic girls to illustrate the article). Though people who write for right-wing newspapers, like Mona Charen, pit African-Americans against Asian-Americans with Asian-American success stories, in Oakland, California, Samoans have a higher school dropout rate than blacks. And what about white students? How do they do when separated from the hundreds of millions of dollars their parents shell out for SAT coaches? There is an operation in Berkeley, California, that promises that your child will score 900 points on the SAT. For $5,000. When compared with the performance of students from other "developed" countries, American students do poorly. Recently they ranked fifteenth in math scores out of sixteen countries and sixteenth out of sixteen in science scores. Maybe this is the reason why the higher the family income, the higher the test scores. How do white suburban kids do deprived of an ability to cheat, a pattern that has been documented by the *New York Times* and the *Wall Street Journal*?

The nation faces a crisis in reading and writing, but does what all nations do, dumps the crisis on a scapegoat. In this country, African-Americans are the permanent scapegoat. Tarred and feathered. Digitally and electronically lynched. While the media and the politicians were casting blame on inner-city youth for the social problems occurring among that age group, I pointed to the violence occurring among suburban or white youth in a *New York Times* op-ed published in 1994.

I said that school violence in the suburbs was similar to that in the inner city in most measures. When the op-ed was printed, the word "most" was changed to "some." My facts were based upon a study that was originally published in the *Times*. Maybe if the media had studied violence in the suburbs as much as obeying their marketing strategy, which holds that you can make money by depicting blacks in a bad light, perhaps we could have predicted Columbine and the numerous school shootings in white schools that have occurred since then. But dumping on blacks and hiding the social pathologies of whites is nothing new in the American media or in American culture in general.

This was a pattern noticed by W. E. B. DuBois during the early part of the last century. In 1926 he said of DuBose Heyward, the librettist for *Porgy and Bess*, that Heyward "writes beautifully of the black Charleston underworld. But why does he do this? Because he cannot do a similar thing for the white people of Charleston, or they would drum him out of town. The only chance he had to tell the truth of pitiful human degradation was to tell it of colored people. . . .

In other words, the white public today demands from its artists, literary and pictorial, racial pre-judgment which deliberately distorts Truth and Justice, as far as colored races are concerned, and it will pay for no other."

I feel that the same is happening with the issue of literacy among the nation's young people. Black kids are being scapegoated for their reading levels when the problem is widespread. What's expected of black and white students is captured in the film *Finding Forrester* in which a black youth clutches a basketball so much that you wonder whether it's another part of his anatomy. This young man is congratulated because he can parrot the lines of nineteenth-century white English writers. In another film, *Dangerous Minds*, it is proposed that if you introduced two white poets to black and Hispanic students, they will see the light. Both of these notions are carryovers from the old missionary notion of education. Take the savage and show him Western culture and he will become enlightened. Jefferson and Washington were always agonizing over the lack of "enlightenment" among the Native Americans. If they'd just become "enlightened," we wouldn't have to exterminate them, our founding fathers proposed. The Cherokee accepted this challenge and were driven from their lands anyway. But this notion of using the classroom to civilize the savage dies hard.

Mona Charen, a professional critic of black people, wants blacks to read Jane Austin. McWorther assures his white readers that he is acquainted with "Western classics." About the time that John H. McWhorter's book appeared, it was reported that a poetry reading sponsored by a group called Youth Speaks had sold out. Youth Speaks is a group of blacks and descendants of indigenous people (referred to as Hispanics by the census) who sponsor Hip Hop poets in local readings. They've been able to draw youth to their readings from countries as far away as Bosnia and Zimbabwe. Last year Youth Speaks held a national festival that drew young people from all over the world. What gives? Black and indigenous people are doing badly in SAT scores, but are flocking to poetry readings. I think that it shows that students will do well if exposed to a literature written by someone from their own background.

Students get turned on to reading and writing when they see their fellow students doing it and when the material has something to do with their lives and the material is interesting. This is not only true of black and Hispanic students but white students as well. It's the obligation of the teacher to introduce into the classroom the techniques that Hip Hoppers and others have used to attract students to writing poetry. These techniques could be used in other fields. I heard a rapper, RS1, deliver a complicated lecture about the subject of biology to some "disadvantaged" students. They were riveted. When his time was up, they asked for more.

I've taught at the University of California at Berkeley for over thirty years and the majority of my students have been middle- and upper-class white students. For the first few years, I used the works of so-called "major" writers to introduce the techniques of writing. One can see the effects of the *Finding Forrester* style of education on these students. When they enter college, their notions of writing are reflected by the stories and poetry they submit when they enter my class. They believe that writing is something that people engaged in hundreds of years ago, and their writing styles include language that has nothing to do with contemporary life. If I were to name the writer whom most of the freshmen imitate, it would probably be Edgar Allen Poe, hands down.

Apparently none of the students' high school teachers had acquainted them with the revolution in modern writing that's almost 100 years old. My students are surprised to learn that the language of everyday life can be transformed into art. Hispanic and black students face another bind. Ninety percent of public school teachers are white, and most of those are white women. So it's highly unlikely that students from those backgrounds will have been introduced to a work by a black writer, unless it's of the kind that blames black males for all of the problems of the Republic. Even with black-male-bashing literature, the selection of authors is limited to a few.

I studied literature written by white men for most of my formal education, but it wasn't until I left the university and took a job in a library that I came in contact with a writer named James Baldwin. Baldwin showed me that someone from my background was capable of writing. I had written some stories in college, but it was James Baldwin's example that convinced me that a black writer could be published. I've heard writers from other ethnic groups say the same thing. Hispanic and Asian-American and Native American writers have been influenced by the example of someone from their background writing. Similarly, I found that my students were very respectful of the major and great writers, but when I began to mix these writers with those works by students from previous classes, their performance rose significantly. I encouraged students to write about subjects that interested them, whether it be a television series like *Star Trek,* or pop icons like Madonna or Michael Jackson.

Students began to write in their evaluations that mine was the most interesting literature class that they were taking; some said that it was the best course they'd studied at the university. Here are some of the assignments I used.

The initial efforts by my students are usually airy and cosmic, with much fuzzy thinking. I try to anchor them and so I have them write about a city, or a town, emphasizing landmarks and characteristics that make the town unique. For models, I use Carl Sandburg's *Chicago*, Richard Hugo's *Port Townsend*, and Jim Gustafson's *The Idea of Detroit*.

Most of my students write autobiographical work in which the first person is usually them. I get them out of their minds with an assignment that challenges them to write from the point of view of a vegetable or fruit. For this assignment, I use Al Young's poem written from the point of view of a tomato. Another assignment is for them to take the point of view of the opposite sex.

Frustrated with the lack of textbooks that would cover the kind of assignments that I had developed and the failure of textbooks in print to include works that reflect the upheaval in American writing that's occurred since the 1960s, I accepted an offer from Harper-Collins to develop one of my own. In addition to four books of which I was general editor, I was also contracted to assemble a textbook that would, I thought, be designed to reflect my thinking about American writing, with emphasis on the most experimental and inclusive. The four volumes were published as the *American Literary Mosaic Series*. They were *African-American Literature*, edited by Al Young; *Hispanic American Literature*, edited by Nick Kanellos; *Asian American Literature*, edited by Shawn Wong; and *Native American Literature*, edited by Gerald Vizenor. Some of the problems faced by these editors, whom I'd chosen, in dealing with New York editors were a precursor of things to come. The white editors in New York were of the kind who hadn't a clue about literature produced in this country except from that written by whites. They were the kind of people who should sue the institutions from which they received their degrees for reparations for keeping them in mental bondage. On top of that, they demonstrated the arrogance of some whites when dealing with individuals of different backgrounds. By their being white, they felt that they knew more about the cultures of my editors than the editors themselves. (It was like Martina Hingis telling the Williams family that she didn't think Venus and Serena Williams had experienced racism in the world of tennis, suggesting that Hingis knows racism when she sees it. Maybe she will be invited to join the Civil Rights Commission, where she can join Abigail Thernstrom in deciding that whenever blacks charge racism, they're seeing things that aren't there.)

One New York editor tried to advise Nick Kanellos, the leading publisher of Hispanic literature in this country, about the contents of his volume. The editor wanted him to include Zane Grey. Kanellos answered that this person trying to advise him about Hispanic literature was like someone trying to advise Jimmy Carter about raising peanuts. Gerald Vizenor, the Native American professor who edited that volume, had many run-ins with these arrogant editors and several times he threatened to quit the project. He insisted that all of the contents of his volume be written by Native American authors. The editors wanted to include white translators and anthropologists whose work some Native American authors consider offensive.

I called my textbook from *Totem to Rap, 10,000 Years of American Writing,* from the totem poles of the Tlingit tribes of the Northwest to the Hip-Hop poetry of today. It would be a volume that would include African-Americans as well as Anglo-Americans, beat, proletariat, imagist feminist, and gay poets. It would include Wallace Stevens as well as Tex Ritter and Dolly Parton. Country western, Rock and Roll, and Tin Pan Alley. The book went out for review several times and the responses from some of the reviewers were ignorant.

Typical was an evaluation from a professor who complained that the volume was absent white writers. Over 50 percent of the writers in the volume were white. The other silly rule that the textbook industry has is that 60 percent of the contents of each new textbook should be works that duplicate the flagship textbooks currently on the market.

The contract for *Totem to Rap* was signed in the early 1990s. Since then, the original editor has left for another company and the original publisher has been bought out twice, I think. The contract is now with Pearson and lies dormant.

At this point in my career, I've come to the conclusion that the problem of literacy, a problem that afflicts students of all races and classes in our society, is a problem having not to do with the intellectual inferiority of the students, or their willingness to learn, or peer group pressure, or any of the other ghosts and hobgoblins afflicting the so-called public discourse, which is usually led by operatives and proxy intellectuals. Instead the problem lies with what is taught, how it's taught, and who teaches it. (Update: Thunder's Mouth Press will publish the poetry section of *From Totem to Rap* in 2003.)

—An earlier version of this essay was delivered to the National Council of Teachers of English meeting, Birmingham, Alabama, March 31, 2001

CHAPTER 14

Progress

IN ORDER TO JUSTIFY ITS PROGRAMS, NASA, IN ITS BROCHURES,
describes the Earth as a dying planet, a fact that, for them, justifies
colonizing the universe. Given the mess that's been made of this
planet in the name of progress, you can understand why, in many
science fiction movies, the goal of the invaders is to destroy the
Earth, lest this progress be extended to their neighborhoods. Many
say that we are reaching the point of no return, beyond which the
salvaging of the planet will be impossible, and a few years ago, a
number of Nobel laureates signed an urgent declaration warning
about human-influenced climate change. Their claims are dismissed as hysterical by spokespersons employed by the fossil-fuel
industry, which has undertaken the kind of public relations campaign that led to the defeat of Hillary Clinton's health proposals.

Another environmentalist warned that at our rate of growth less
food will be grown in the next forty years than in the last 8,000.
These prophecies and others lend credence to Richard Leakey's
warning that man is on the brink of his extinction. He said that
"global warming, loss of the rain forests, industrial pollution of the
waterways, depletion of the ozone layer, and the spread of AIDS
were among the factors that were a potential threats to the species."

How did we reach this disaster? I would suggest that it can be
traceable to a perverted notion of progress, a word that, according

to the *American Heritage Dictionary*, is chiefly British. England was the scene of the industrial revolution, which led to the chemical revolution and other dangerous "progressive" solutions, mostly heralded for their benefits to mankind, or as "time-saving devices," and for their ability to make our lives more convenient. The countries where these revolutions have taken place hold them over the rest of the nations as proof of their superiority. If you don't have this gadgetry, it is said, then you are "underdeveloped" or even "backward."

On the day that Rover landed on Mars and began transmitting pictures, white sportscasters were gloating over the fact that Mike Tyson had chomped off part of Evander Holyfield's ear. The juxtaposition of those images said it all. While white men are reaching the stars, the rest of us are cannibals. We're still saying "B'Wana" in the Tarzan movies.

Even though black scientists are responsible for inventing some of the most avant-garde of space equipment, Norman Mailer, in his book *Fire On The Moon*, said that such space shots emasculated we primitives. (After the O. J. trial, Norman Mailer said that African-Americans supported the defendant because we are less rational than whites. If a "progressive" thinks this way, you can imagine how the others think.)

But as our fish develop sores and die as result of pollution, as our air becomes dirtier, as the ozone is depleted over the Antarctic, our devotion to progress can be viewed as a Faustian bargain. All one has to do is visit the Peace Museum at Hiroshima to understand that one person's progress is another person's hell.

The twentieth century has witnessed a marriage of heaven and hell. Millions of people have lived in a style that was only available to the elites of a former time, indeed, only to kings and queens. Mass production of inexpensive books has made literacy more available to the average person than it was to Shakespeare, who lived in a time when the best books were locked away by the elite. You can walk up Telegraph Avenue in Berkeley, or Broadway near Lincoln Center in New York, and sidewalk hawkers will sell you literary classics for a few dollars and used CDs of Beethoven's last quartets and John Coltrane playing soprano saxophone for a little more.

State subsidies make dance and theater available to millions and, with search engines, more information can be had in your home than was available to colleges and universities in the last thousand years.

Great strides have been made in medicine, sparing millions the scourge of diseases that in a former time devastated whole populations, and incredible moral and political revolutions were wrought by Ghandi and Martin Luther King Jr. without their firing a single shot.

But while men and women have behaved brilliantly in this century, they have also been stupid, venal, vile, and even wicked. Even though the so-called Cold War has ended, the manufacturing of newer, more sophisticated nuclear weapons continues. Scenes of horror and mass destruction and extermination are broadcast on television, interrupted only by the hawking of products. Mass murders in Indonesia, Rwanda, and Cambodia vie with those of World War I and II in their enormity. Jason Epstein says that these grim atrocities may only be a preparation for even more horrible holocausts that will take place in the twenty-first century. So inevitable is human progress that perhaps by the middle of the twenty-first century each person will own a custom-made mass grave. The fashion industry will vanish. All that will be required is a bio-hazard suit and an oxygen tank.

In the United States, plagues, both natural and manmade, devastate whole neighborhoods and populations, and even though the media flatter the entity they refer to as "white America," by blaming these catastrophes on the lack of moral character among the black and brown populations, social pathologies extend to the suburbs as well. While the black "out-of-wedlock rate" has declined drastically, that of the white population is soaring (yet black pathology merchants from think tanks and journalism still write about rising out-of-wedlock rates when even Ben Wattenberg of the American Enterprise Institute says it's not so).

The *Philadelphia Inquirer* reported that heroin abuse in the suburbs is skyrocketing. Yet, the media continue to blame the drug trade on black foot soldiers, which is like blaming drugstore clerks for the phen-fen diet pill scandal, and a whole industry has emerged, based upon the scolding of blacks and devoted to the idea that racism no longer exists. One of those who've hit the jackpot is a *New Yorker* writer, Joe Klein. He says that so impoverished are the moral values of the inner cities that the areas should be turned over to the churches. When is the last time that Joe Klein read the Bible, where, if you really want to read some invective, check out Jesus Christ holding forth on hypocrisy. Joe Klein was one of the biggest liars of the 1990s. He's not the only one. One of the governors who has been praised for cutting "immoral" welfare recipients off food stamps and other subsidies made the short list for vice presidential nominees during the last campaign. His name was dropped from the list when it was revealed that he was supporting his mistress from his wife's bank account. An elitist magazine editor who recommended to blacks that they adhere to bourgeoisie values was found to be a dedicated cocaine addict, and the founder of supply-side economics, who used to go on *Wall Street Week* and scorn money spent on social programs, was so spaced out on cocaine that his wife had to petition for the right to control his estate. I could go on.

This century has proven that technology, arrogance, and ignorance are a lethal concoction. Now the government tells us that the nuclear fallout from its crazy tests has infected thousands with cancer. Forty years after the fact they tell us that poor blacks and whites were used in plutonium experiments. Maybe forty years from now they will admit that they cooperated with organized crime and international hoodlums who brought drugs into our country, murdering the souls of millions and now not only destroying the neighborhoods that were targeted but the suburbs. They tell us that people who look like them are the brightest and the best: Aristotle, whose views on women are stupid, or Diderot, a racist, and Voltaire, an anti-Semite and a racist. As soon as Microsoft, the state of the art in cyberspace, went online Microsoft had to apologize for referring to Indians as savages, a good example of the canyon that exists between our knowledge of objects and our knowledge of one another. Maybe our truncated knowledge of the world is the result of the Great Books cannon including not one Asian, or African, or European woman.

Once in a while we get a glimpse of the philosophy guiding the corporate-owned politicians who sell us their masters' final product gleaming in the political showrooms. What's behind the Contract for America, Proposition 187, Proposition 209, the growing prison industry, the welfare bill, mandatory sentencing, the prohibition against clean needles, and reduction and elimination of services for the elderly and the disabled?

The American Psychological Association was about to honor Raymond B. Cattell until the Anti-Defamation League reminded the group of some of his racist writings. Cattell believes that "poverty and disease are part of the natural selection process that keeps a race healthy. Modern social welfare simply abolishes the checks natural selection imposes on biological systems." Cattell and his friends regard Christianity as "a denial of the urge to evolution" encouraging "the increase of the unfit." How do we deal with the unfit? By using "genthanasia," a "phasing out" in which a moribund culture is ended, by education and birth. Immigration for Cattell only draws "people of low genetic quality." The American Psychological Association nonetheless saluted Cattell for his "lifetime contribution in the public interest."

Cattell, who said in 1994 that Hitler actually shared many values of the average American, may have tapped into the zeitgeist. Charles Murray's book *The Bell Curve*, which includes similar arguments and was partially financed by the Pioneer Fund, whose Nazi ties have been documented, was favorably received even by the *New York Times Book Review*, which we all thought was a liberal outfit. Even more disturbing was that Murray's collaborator was a Jewish-American psychologist, R. J. Herrnstein.

It's hard to disagree with the animal photographer Peter Beard, who, while lamenting the vanishing elephant herds, said that humans are the most greedy and selfish animal in the animal kingdom. Humans are the animal that began the twentieth century with an ugly circus of carnage called World War I, and, toward the end of the century was speculating about how to phase out unwanted groups through genthanasia. To some, that's progress.

—**An earlier version of this essay was published in "How We Want to Live," edited by Susan Shreve**

CHAPTER 15

Marketing "Urban Nihilism"

FLATTERING NEW WHITES BY DISPARAGING BLACKS HAS BECOME big business for television and newspapers and for an army of think tank intellectuals like D'Nesh D'souza, who has earned millions of dollars for pushing some of the same theories as John C. Calhoun, a staunch defender of slavery, and for Hollywood, an old hand at raising lynch mobs against blacks (but not as dedicated as the newspaper industry, which has not only inspired riots and lynchings, but gave instructions to the mob on where to go and what equipment to bring). Billions have been made by invaders from the suburbs who've used themes from "high-crime" districts (Wall Street? Capitol Hill? Silicon Valley?) as a basis for television series like *Hill Street Blues* and *Homicide* and *The Wire*. Documentary film, television, and radio producers compete for Corporation for Public Television and Ford Foundation funds that will enable them to put project blacks on exhibit the way that the anthropologist A. L. Kroeber exhibited Ishi the Indian. One show, public radio's *This American Life,* produced by Ira Glass, is particularly offensive.

The white audiences, who can't get enough of this stuff, seem to need a middle person, a fellow white, to cover this material for them, a trend we've seen from the white minstrels to what James

Weldon Johnson called "The Negro Delineators" of today, and although some black filmmakers have made some money from depicting life in the hood, little of this money has ended up in the pockets of black writers. Some of our most well-known white novelists have cashed in on what Richard Price calls "urban nihilism," the fancy phrase for the same old "Catfish Row." Price, who was, at one time, on the way to becoming a great novelist, decided somewhere along the line to go for the money. He gets paid millions for penning such neo-plantation lines as "Besides, ain't no criminals here . . . Shit, you all ain't even *done* nothin'. No stickup mens, no muggers, killers. I don't truck with that. I don't take on nobody with violence on they jacket. You motherfuckers are making it the only way they let poor niggers make it. On the street. Hustlin'."

Du Bose Heyward would be proud.

Black male writers were left for literary roadkill in the late eighties, because they were confronted by a powerful feminist movement that designated the black male as a mascot for male evil. Black critics, who saw an opportunity and sales in women's studies and consumers, signed on to this attitude. Even Emmett Till, who was murdered and mutilated for whistling to get attention from some white store owners, following his mother's instructions that he do so when seized by an episode of stuttering, became, in the eyes of some feminists, a misogynist. It's a tribute to the resiliency of black male novelists that they continued to produce important works of fiction despite this cultural revolution that sought to steamroll over them. (And though it's been announced stridently that the only important development since the civil rights movement has been black women writers, most of the serious black women writers I know remain in obscurity or unpublished.) John Wideman, Charles Johnson, Clarence Major, Ernest Gaines, and others have been fortunate enough to receive recognition. One of the country's best writers, William Melvin Kelley, shows that he still has his chops, publishing excellent short stories from time to time. Al Young and Cecil Brown persist. Amiri Baraka continues to write so well that he can even make Communist theory sound interesting. Well-deserved attention has been paid to such younger writers as Chris Farley and Trey Ellis, Jeff Allen and Colson Whitehead. Others of a younger generation, such as John Keene and the Fiction Collective's Phillip Lewis, write on without the recognition they deserve. So disgusted has Darius James become to the reception to his work that he has chosen exile, finding Berlin, a place so dangerous for blacks that some have begun carrying weapons, preferable to New York, where Rudy Giuliani's Street Crimes Unit is allowed to run berserk.

Paul Beatty, more than any other black male writer under forty, has received the recognition that has been denied the others of his generation. It helps to have a powerful patron. Mine was Langston Hughes. Michele Wallace and Toni Morrison have identified Gloria Steinem as the driving force behind the success of some black literary Divas. Allen Ginsberg championed the work of Paul Beatty, and Ginsberg was right.

Beatty is one of the most talented young writers to come along in many years. He has the guts and verve and genius of a Tiger Woods on paper. His writing skills are extraordinary. The only problem with the new novel is the subject matter. When Claude Brown wrote his brilliant *Manchild in the Promised Land*, "'hood" material was fresh. Now, with cable competing with the networks for the millions who are fascinated with the lifestyles of the kind of characters found in this book, their colorful Ebonics, and their living on the "existential" edge, with the commercialization of rap and Hip Hop, which has resulted in a glut, with twenty-four-hour installments of *Cops* and exposure to the brothers and sisters who appear on Jerry Springer, a novelist who covers this familiar territory had better be original. In some ways Beatty meets that test, his urban nihilists being far more nuanced than those of Tom Wolfe, whose black characters have less of a vocabulary than your Stanford laboratory monkey or of Quentin Torrentino, whose films include direct quotes from *The Birth of a Nation*.

With his character Fariq, Beatty introduces the 'hood intellectual, a type ignored by the white tourist writers. Fariq says: "That's why a prudent motherfucker like me has an IRA account, some short-term T-Bills, a grip invested in long-term corporate bonds and high-risk foreign stock. Shit, the twenty-first-century nigger gots to have a diversified portfolio—never know when you gon' have a rainy day." But, for the most part, many of the situations and images belong to the cliché hall of fame: "Rats scaled mountains of trash bags." Also, the book should gain an entry in the Guiness Book of Records for the number of times the words "nigger" and "motherfucker" are used. After a white woman psychiatrist used the term "motherfucker" in Woody Allen's *Deconstructing Harry*, maybe the word should be retired.

All the pathologies that have been ascribed exclusively to the urban nihilists are displayed by Beatty, whose narrator speaks a pretentious English as a way of separating himself from the homeboys. "Yolanda saw her reflection framed by the sentimental bromide and succumbed to the wanton manipulation that is romance." Added to the traditional pathologies that we hear about to death are homophobia and anti-Semitism, even though the typical perpetrators of violence against gays and Jews are white men.

Beatty even introduces a black rabbi named Spencer Jefferson Jr., who becomes the Big Brother to one of the novel's main characters. After a lengthy introduction, most of the time this character just hangs around, there being no reason for him to be included. Winston, and his friend Fariq (a combination of Farrakhan and Malik) are the kind of characters that people whom think tanks pay good money for recycling the same old stereotypes might call "super-predators." Black teens are "wolf packs" and are often located within "mugging distance" of passersby. The plot centers around Winston "Tuffy" Forshay's attempt to become a councilman. The plot never thickens; in fact, it becomes thinner as the book proceeds.

Just as some of the scenes and images have been done before, so have some of the targets been done to death. Neoconservatives like Richard Bernstein, who enjoyed Beatty's first book, *White Boy Shuffle*, endorsed another pathology show, *Straight Out Of Brook-*

lyn, and believe that Western civilization is under an assault from multiculturalism, will enjoy the attacks on the 60s, black nationalism, and black writing (a hit made earlier by the late Bernard Malamud with his ridiculous character Willie Spearmint). The Nation of Islam, the Hip Hoppers, those who helped Beatty into prominence before he was taken uptown, also come under attack. (After spending about half of my life reading poetry, most of which I didn't understand, I welcome the drive, energy, clarity, and social protest of the Hip Hoppers.) There are also some attacks on the white left; talk about beating a dead horse. There are also some hilarious lines about "sisterhood" writing, but, in some of the dialogue between Winston Tuff and his lover, Yolanda, the author shows that he is also capable of writing the kind of sappy lines that have Oprahized the black literary scene, books in which saintly black women triumph over black male demons.

His characters are, for the most part, police line-up chic. The main character, Winston, is the sort of black male whom people at the Manhattan Institute must salivate over. The guy is a nasty piece of work. The opening scene finds Winston waking in an apartment that has been shot up by some crack dealers. He's there because he was hired as an enforcer for a rival of the shooters. His foul career doesn't end there. He's also a chain snatcher, a knifer, and when left to attend some noisy children, keeps them quiet by knocking them out with chloroform.

What salvages this book is the writing. Beatty has an extraordinary eye for detail and the book reads like a Vermeer painting, but good writing isn't enough. Beatty needs a vision. He sounds as if he's read Henry Louis Gates Jr., the "intellectual entrepreneur" and "capitalist" who instructed black artists on how to become as rich as he. The formula seems to be that one writes nothing that would alienate white consumers, selling them guilt-free products like Gates's conclusion that it was Africans who engineered themselves across the Atlantic in the first place, while the slave ship captains looked on, helplessly. The blueprint for "The Fourth Renaissance" is that of blaming the situation of black characters not on racism, but on "behavior."

If Beatty continues to write work like *Tuff,* he will be embraced by the same crowd that embraced Ralph Ellison, whose book *Invisible Man* ridicules some of the same targets Beatty does. Ralph Ellison was partied around by the New York literary crowd like a museum piece for forty years and, like his literary sons, was used to demean the literary achievements of other black writers. Though those who champion Ellison—people whose knowledge of literature is confined to that written by white males—cast the writer as a victim of verbal abuse from those whom they call "black militants," the late Larry Neal's criticism of Ellison's work is very cogent. Neal said that the younger generation of black writers had little understanding of some of the issues with which Ellison dealt—issues involving radical politics of 1930s and 1940s New York. There was also a difference in aesthetics separating Ellison from the younger writers. While Ellison and members of his generation used a closeted, opaque prose, perhaps chilled by McCarthyism, the younger generation felt free to tell it like it was.

Paul Beatty could become the new Ralph Ellison. Another possibility is for Beatty to write the kind of book that would make those who still set the cultural agenda for the country uncomfortable, as the late John O. Killens did and as John A. Williams continues to do. Williams's latest novel, *Clifford's Blues,* is about black concentration camps. He had to get an alternative publisher because New York editors refused to believe that blacks were placed in concentration camps during the Nazi period. The critics have said that John A. Williams should stick to writing about civil rights and lynchings. But, fortunately for us, he won't be hooded. John A. Williams hasn't gotten rich but he can face himself in the mirror each morning.

—An earlier version of this review
appeared in the *Village Voice,*
April 10, 2000

CHAPTER 16

Was 9/11 the First Terrorist Attack on American Soil?

Though the disenfranchisement of black Americans might have been the main issue during the recent presidential election in Florida, *Brill's Content* reported that few black commentators were invited by the networks to talk about it. This was also true during the aftermath of the attack on the World Trade Center. What we got was analyzing and pontificating by the same wealthy white men. While doing so, they exhibited the arrogant attitude that is partially responsible for hatred against the United States in many parts of the world. The typical image of blacks during the aftermath of the attack was that of a nurturer. On the networks, blacks were shown comforting people or singing hymns. Even the *New Yorker*, which is supposed to be hip, ran an illustration of a black woman hugging somebody, while the serious responses were made by white writers. The *New York Times* printed three articles about how writers past and present have treated such calamities. No black writers were mentioned and even though all three articles were written by women, only a few token white women were cited. If the country goes to war, black men and women will do a substantial amount of the dying. So where does one go to discover how black soldiers feel? How they think?

Whether fiction is dead might be a dinner party conversation on the Upper West Side or in Santa Monica but, for some black men, fiction is one of the few means by which they can tell their story. It took John A. Williams and John O. Killens to write about the experiences of black men during World War II. In his *And Then We Heard The Thunder*, Killens, like black male writers of the past, exposed one of the cherished myths of the culture—that "the Greatest Generation" was all virtuous and fought a war to save democracy. In his book, members of that generation are shown lynching black soldiers, denying them civil rights, and treating their enemies better than their black comrades.

Anthony Grooms, with his first novel, *Bombingham*, joins a distinguished group of writers who have written about the experience of black soldiers in Vietnam. They include Lorenzo Thomas, Yusef Komunyakaa, Arthur Flowers, and George Davis. Grooms is well aware of the omission of the experience of black soldiers in war in popular culture. His character, Walter Burke, says: "I had seen *From Here to Eternity*, but I had never known that black men had died at Pearl Harbor; I didn't even think blacks were allowed into Pearl Harbor. Nowhere in our history books did I see a black soldier, or on statues."

The novel alternates between Walter Burke in combat, described in horrifying detail, writing a letter to the parents of his dead comrade, Haywood, and flashes back to Walter Burke as a boy, coming of age during the civil rights struggle of 1950s Birmingham, Alabama. These public conflicts are played against the private turmoil of the Burke family. A stubborn and stern mother, who believes that faith healers will cure her cancer, fights with the father, a high school science teacher, whose approach to life is "scientific." Their quarrels rip the family apart so that relatives have to be summoned to assume control of the household. This gives Grooms a chance to present the viewpoints of three generations of blacks about the growing militancy of Birmingham blacks as well to let them settle old scores between themselves.

As in the case of many black families, a terrible injustice, committed in the past, haunts every generation. In this book, a grandfather died in jail after being falsely accused of rape by a white woman. As the young Burke and his sister Josie join their young friend, Lamar, in the demonstrations, they are scolded by their conservative parents, in a rare instance of agreement. Burke's father says, "Listen, Son, it is very important that you don't get involved in that tomfoolery. It could ruin what chances you have. It's dangerous." His dying mother is a proud segregationist who barely contains her contempt for whites: "We never saw any white people, so we were just who we were. We didn't have to pretend one way or the other. No delusions about 'overcoming.'" Both Josie and her brother defy their parents and conservative school officials by joining Dr. King and the demonstrators. Even their dog, Bingo, gets into the act, killed after a courageous confrontation with a police dog.

Bombingham is constructed so well that it could be used as a textbook in writing classes. It's a perfect traditional novel. There are characters whom you feel for. The scenes are so vivid that they could be staged without any adaptation. Their speeches tell you as much about the characters as the excellent descriptions. Well-crafted novels are common; however, Grooms brings more to his book. His talent and persistence is evident in this virtuoso performance in which a variety of fictional techniques are on full display. He has the rare ability to transport the reader to those times about which he writes. We even get the odors and the sounds, the popular music and the television shows of the 1950s. Grooms's battlefield writing brings the war home to the reader: "The thirty-calibers picked up again; the mud became soupy with blood and piss; the sun became hotter, and then air filled with biting flies. There was the smell of open bowels, smoke, and oil. The guns whined and popped incessantly."

The book is called *Bombingham* because in Birmingham

"Bombings were so common that the blacks gave it that name." Grooms writes: "The Birmingham Klan was too sophisticated to toss a rope over a tree limb." Contrary to the comments of one of the elitist commentators, who was burdened with the task of filling up time during the week of September 11, terrorism on American soil is not rare. The Klan, which was begun as a Confederate guerrilla movement, has waged a terrorist campaign against black people since the end of the Civil War. Blacks in Tulsa, Oklahoma, and in Philadelphia have been bombed from the air.

Nowadays the Klan's rhetoric has been co-opted by talk-show hosts. Why on earth does the Klan need their website NiggerWatch (which gets a lot of its material from the mainstream media) when it has the Don Imus show?

In Anthony Grooms's *Bombingham* the heavy is played by Bull Connor, the oafish chief of public safety whose brutal treatment of the demonstrators provoked worldwide outrage and sympathy for Dr. King's cause. "Bull Connor looked much less like a bull than he did a hog."

It's ironic that nonviolent institutions have picked up where Bull Connor, the head of the vicious Birmingham police force, and his associates left off. They are more subtle than Connor and, unlike the man whom Grooms calls "the archenemy himself," capable of influencing public policy.

—An earlier version of this essay
appeared in the *Village Voice*,
December 4, 2001

CHAPTER 17

Ed Turner and Friends

SO MUCH RACIST FICTION IS BEING WRITTEN NOWADAYS THAT for one book to be the most racist is really going some. *The Turner Diaries*, by William L. Pierce, who writes under the pseudonym of Andrew MacDonald, is that novel.

This book was a sort of how-to manual for Timothy McVeigh, the man who bombed the federal building in Oklahoma, an action foreshadowed by *The Turner Diaries*. Among the book's other actions are a commando attack on the *Washington Post*, the forced expulsion of blacks, Chicanos, and other "mongrel" races from Los Angeles, and a nuclear attack on Israel. For the Organization, Ed Turner's white supremacist group, dedicated to waging all-out war against the Zionist-Occupied Government (ZOG), the First Amendment is less important than the Second. So enthusiastic was McVeigh about *The Turner Diaries* that he sold it at gun shows. Though the media have cited the book as McVeigh's inspiration, few journalists have explored its contents. All of their wrath seems to be reserved for Rap and Hip Hop music, but, as far as I know, nobody ever bombed a federal building or shot up a Jewish day care center because they were inspired by rap or Hip Hop music.

Ed Turner's resentment has been building up against the System, which, according to the Organization, serves the interest of Jews and blacks and enforces its will with the hated Equality Police.

The revolution erupts with the passage of the Cohen Act. This act outlaws all private ownership of firearms in the United States. In *The Turner Diaries*, the Cohen Act is merely an excuse for "groups of Blacks forcing their way into White homes to rob and rape." The main obsession of this book is "race mixing." The black males rape white women while the Jewish males lure them into white slavery. What happens to these girls? "Most are confined in certain exclusive clubs in New York where the wealthy go to satisfy strange and perverted appetites. Some, it is rumored, are eventually sold to a Satanist club and painfully dismembered in gruesome rituals."

Puerto Ricans, Chicanos, "kinky-haired" Middle Easterners, and others are considered "mongrel" as well. "The cosmopolitan racial goulash one finds in every American metropolitan area these days" are among the enemies of the Organization. Even "rednecks," those who would seem to be the natural allies of the Organization, come in for criticism. Two of its members are killed when they come in contact with "good ol' boys," who have no use for people who wanted to "overthrow the gummint." White conservatives are considered race traitors, as are other whites who don't share the Organization's vision. A "responsible conservative" loses both his legs and suffers severe internal injuries after members of the Organization wire a bomb to the ignition of his car.

But none of the groups are hated as much as blacks and Jews, and between these groups, the Jews are the most hated. When the blacks are not raping white women, on every other page it seems, they commit acts of cannibalism. When the Organization's military arm expels the blacks and Jews from Los Angeles, they stumble upon a scene that the blacks have left behind: "whites were dragged from their cars, taken into a nearby Black restaurant, butchered, cooked, and eaten." But in comparison to the crimes of which Ed Turner and the Organization accuse the Jews, these are mere pranks.

Jews are considered to have poisoned Western civilization, no less. "If the White nations of the world had not allowed themselves to become subject to the Jew, to Jewish ideas, to the Jewish spirit, this war would not be necessary." The author of this book argues that World War II was a struggle between Jews and Germans and the United States joined the wrong side. In another passage, he describes white men as "a mass man; a member if the great, brainwashed proletariat; a herd animal; a true democrat," who has been corrupted by "the flood of Jewish-materialist propaganda in which they have been submerged practically all their lives."

Timothy McVeigh considered the children and infants killed in the nursery located inside the federal building to be "collateral damage." He probably got that from this book, because if you're making a war against the System, innocent whites, those whom you are trying to save from Jews and blacks, must be killed too. Makes sense, no?

Pierce puts it this way: "No, talk of 'innocents' has no meaning. We must look at our situation collectively, in a race-wide sense. We must understand that our race is like a cancer patient undergoing drastic surgery in order to save his life. There is no sense in asking whether the tissue being cut out is 'innocent' or not." Toward the end of the novel, when an apocalyptic nuclear war between the races occurs, even one fifth of the Organization's members are killed. Such martyrdom is required by the Organization, whose members must defend a white race gone "soft, city-bred, brainwashed" and seduced by material goods. "Slavery is the just and proper state for a people who have grown as soft, self-indulgent, careless, credulous, and befuddled as we have."

Buried beneath the cant and invective is a love story. It's reminiscent of the romance between the lovers in George Orwell's *1984*, the novel that is most similar to *The Turner Diaries*. Individuals are overwhelmed by an impersonal System. The System is Big Brother. Though one would expect Turner and his girlfriend to subscribe to the entire right-wing agenda, their arrangement is not likely to meet the approval of the Rev. Jerry Falwell. "We are unwilling to regard our growing relationship as purely sexual, bearing no obligations, neither are we inclined to formalize it yet." The Christian church is also on Pierce's enemies list. Why? "The Jewish takeover of the Christian churches and corruption of the ministry are now virtually complete."

Pierce's romance writing is awkward. He's no Danielle Steele. He's much better at violence. His main occupation in this book is to hurt people and groups who don't share the views of the Organization. The System hires Israeli and Mafia hitmen to kill members of the Organization. (Jews even control the Mafia, in this book.) When the Organization strikes a Mafia club, more than 400 persons lose their lives. And how does the Utopia that would replace our present "mongrel goulash" look? After the Organization rids Southern California of Chicanos, blacks, and Jews, Ed Turner surveys the Aryan superpersons as they do chores near Santa Barbara. "In the countryside I passed literally hundreds of organized groups of White youngsters, some working in the orchards and fruit groves, others marching along side the road singing, with fruit baskets slung across their shoulders. *They all looked tanned* (my italics) and happy and healthy."

A few years ago, Henry Louis Gates Jr., writing in the *New York Times*, claimed that the last vestiges of anti-Semitism resided in the black community, even though the Anti-Defamation League had released statistics during the same time indicating that anti-Semitism among blacks had declined by 8 percent. Gates's op-ed was sensationalized by the ratings-driven media and reached a national and international audience. When I visited Israel in December 2000, I tried to convince some Israeli intellectuals that every black American wasn't an anti-Semite. I agree with the *Tikkun* publisher, Rabbi Michael Lerner, and Barry Glassner, author of *The Culture of Fear*, that the so-called feud between blacks and Jews has been hyped and that the main enemy of both Jews and blacks is the white right. Still, whatever tensions exist between blacks and Jews could be resolved more easily if racism among some Jews was condemned as harshly as anti-Semitism among some blacks. Gates says that the *New York Times* promised they'd cover the subject of racism among

Jews if Gates condemned black anti-Semitism. However, the op-ed condemning racism among Jews never appeared. *New York Observer* columnist Joe Conason is one of those who has commented about the double standard to which black anti-Semites and Jewish racists are held.

Pierce is aware of these tensions. "Izzy and Sambo are really at one another's throats, tooth and nail, and it is a joy to behold." What's scary about Pierce's vision is that the images of blacks in this book can be found in novels, films, and plays by some Jewish writers and filmmakers. While writing this article, I had a chance to see Steven Spielberg's *Gremlins*. It's obvious who the jazz-loving, break-dancing creatures with black faces and red lips are supposed to represent. These creatures destroy the tranquility of a white town, which resembles the one in *You Can't Take It With You* (1938). The gremlins (blacks) go on a rampage of destruction and murder. Spielberg saved the rape part for *The Color Purple*, in which a black man, named Mr., rapes his stepdaughter. Alice Walker, the author of the novel upon which the film was based, wrote in her book *Stepping into the Same River Twice,* that she found the portrayal offensive. And though Pierce considers feminism "a form of mass psychosis" meant to divide white women from white men, there have been, historically, white feminists who have also subscribed to the myth that the typical rape is interracial rather than intraracial. (Feminist Gloria Steinem said that *The Color Purple* told the truth about black men.) Most women are raped by someone they know, not strangers.

Black rapists can be found in the works of Philip Roth and Saul Bellow, and both writers have included in their works black flashers. In Nazi Germany, Jewish men were accused of raping Aryan women and the typical image of Jewish males by Nazi cartoonists was that of a flasher. Either Roth and Bellow aren't aware of this history, or they're campaigning for admission to the same club to which Pierce belongs. Bellow's statement that the 1960s was defined by a "sexual niggerhood" is pure Pierce.

While black anti-Semites are branded by the media and a stupid remark about Jews, made by basketball player Charles Ward, is
condemned by columnists in the *New York Times* and *The Nation*,
the racism of some Jews is tolerated, or even rewarded, and in
some rare cases given a slight reprimand. Journalist Phil Nobile has
been documenting racist remarks made by Don Imus and his
morning show colleagues for years. Among the sponsors of Imus,
whose show is carried on General Electric's MSNBC, is the *New
York Times*, where the Gates op-ed condemning black anti-Semitism
appeared.(David Remnick, editor of the *New Yorker*, which, under
the editorship of Tina Brown printed an article by Gates accusing
Minister Louis Farrakhan of "unhealthy ideas," accepted an award
from Imus.) In June of last year, Sid Rosenberg, Imus's sports an-
nouncer, said that the Williams sisters were "animals" who should
pose "nude in *National Geographic*." Imus pretended to be upset
and suspended Rosenberg for a few days.

Even some of our leading Jewish intellectuals and historians
aren't immune to the kind of racist attitudes found in *The Turner
Diaries*. Shelby Foote compared the Ku Klux Klan, which has
lynched, murdered, and massacred black people since the end of
the Civil War, with the French Resistance. Sick!

Ed Turner has friends in the theater as well. Seldom has a
young playwright been given so much attention by the *New York
Times* as Rebecca Gilman. Since 1996, she has received forty-one
citations in the newspaper of record. Most of the attention has
been given to her play *Spinning Into Butter*. I caught the play at
Lincoln Center, where I was the only black in the audience. (The
other blacks present in the theater were ushers and concession dis-
pensers.) I could tell from the beginning of the play that it would
be a feminist tract (the white feminist, Sarah, has to tolerate car-
toonish white men and white women who haven't discovered feminism). Gilman's view of the American campus is the kind that one
gets on Fox News. For her and Fox, American campuses are over-
run with political correctness, represented in this play by a pushy

Puerto Rican. The plot centers around a black student who's been the object of a hate crime. He made it up, a plot element that trivializes the hundreds of verbal and physical attacks against blacks, Hispanics, and Asian-Americans that occur on American campuses and are documented in such publications as the *Chronicle of Higher Education.* I sat there, wondering why the *New York Times* would devote such attention to such a clumsy play until some ugly racist speeches occurred in the middle of the play. During this tirade, uttered by Sarah, a privileged white woman who believes her condition to be parallel to that of poor black, brown, and white women, blacks are called "lazy, stupid, loud, abusive, and stinky." ("Lazy," "stupid," and "loud" are repeated.) If these images sounded familiar to me, it's because they're the typical ones you see in the *New York Times,* which associates blacks with welfare, drugs, anti-Semitism, misogyny, crime, and a host of other social ills. Gilman is Jewish and I wondered, when I saw this play, whether she knew that some of the white character's descriptions of blacks were the typical ones used against Jews in a former time, especially Jewish women. "The Ghetto Girl," Jewish women of the turn of the last century, were criticized by Jewish men and Anglo writers for their "vulgarity, lack of social graces, loudness, and garishness," according to the book, *Remembering the Lower East Side: American Jewish Reflections* by Diner, Shandler, and Wenger.

Speilberg, Roth, Bellow, and Gilman aren't the only artists who are pushing some of the same ideas as Pierce. Many of the ideas about race found in the works of Tom Wolfe are consistent with those in *The Turner Diaries.* The thesis of *The Bonfire of the Vanities* was that blacks were destroying New York with the help of Jewish leniency or liberalism. In *The Man In Full,* as close as you're likely to get to the kind of novels that Thomas Dixon (*The Klansman*) used to write, blacks are given to subhuman utterances and mindless violence and a black rapist gets into trouble for raping a white girl.

Not to be outdone, Gore Vidal became very chummy with Timothy McVeigh, before the man who shattered hundreds of lives and murdered men and women and children because he was inspired by Pierce's work was executed. In *The Nation* magazine, Vidal proposed a white Confederacy that would include the United States, Russia, and Europe, the Aryan brotherhood for which McVeigh, in the eyes of his fans, chose martyrdom. Of course, Timothy McVeigh was Irish. Roth, Bellow, Price, Spielberg, David Simon, and other Jewish filmmakers and writers might be interested to know that the Jews on the Lower East Side were once considered such a criminal element that an 1883 edition of the *New York Times* advised respectable citizens to avoid that section of Manhattan.

> The neighborhood where these people live is absolutely impassable for wheeled vehicles other than their pushcarts. If a truck driver tries to get through where their pushcarts are standing they apply to him all kinds of vile and indecent epithets. The driver is fortunate if he gets out of the street without being hit with a stone or having a putrid fish or piece of meat thrown in his face. This neighborhood, peopled almost entirely by the people who claim to have been driven from Poland and Russia, is the eyesore of New York and perhaps the filthiest place on the western continent. It is impossible for a Christian to live there because he will be driven out, either by blows or the dirt and stench. Cleanliness is an unknown quantity to these people. They cannot be lifted up to a higher plane because they do not want to be [similar to the theory about the so-called "black underclass" promoted by neoconservative publications and the Talented Tenth's explanation of black poverty as stemming from the addiction of some blacks to a "culture of poverty"]. If the cholera should ever get among these people, they would scatter its germs as a sower does grain."

Even a book as diabolical as *The Turner Diaries* can serve a purpose. It can give some of our leading intellectuals, commentators, op-ed writers, pundits, think tank moles, and filmmakers a standard by which they can gauge their racial attitudes. It can also pose the question to all European-Americans: has becoming "white" been too high a cost for losing their heritages? A woman who runs an antiracism workshop says that most of her white clients don't know their family trees and are rootless and lost in a sea of whiteness. Timothy McVeigh shows how deadly the consequences of ethnic amnesia can be. He might have thought of himself as an Aryan, but an Irish-American's claiming such status probably induced snickers among some of his "pure-blooded" allies whose Teutonic antecedents once called the Irish "niggers turned inside out."

(Update: William Pierce, the author of *The Turner Diaries,* died on July 23, 2002.)

May 31, 2002

Index